The Very Essence of Massage

Always consult your doctor if in any doubt about your health. If taking medication or treatment from a medical or other complementary practitioner, you should seek their advice before using essential oils or massage as part of a home treatment.

Massage and aromatherapy are complementary therapies and should not replace any existing medication you have been prescribed.

Please read Chapter 3 'Contra-indications' carefully before beginning massage, and Chapter 5 'Using essential oils' before you attempt to use essential oils in your massage.

The author and publisher do not accept responsibility for any problems or any adverse reaction caused by the inappropriate use of oils, the use of poor-quality oils or oils that have been stored incorrectly.

First published in September 1997 by
Likisma Presentations Limited,
Dolphin House, Denington Road,
Wellingborough,
Northants NN8 2QH

Reprinted March 1999

British Library Cataloguing in Publication Data

A catalogue record for this book is available from the British Library.

ISBN 0 9528429 1 2

Printed and bound in Great Britain by
Biddles Ltd, Guildford and King's Lynn

Contents

Acknowledgements

My grateful thanks must first go to my long-suffering partner - not just through the writing of this book, but also for the past 21 years! Lisa Burke of Likisma has provided support and encouragement, which has regularly been needed.

To my wonderful models Nathan, Claire and Angie I say well done and thanks - I know it wasn't always easy for you! My past and present clients and students have been a great source of information and experience, which is much appreciated. An excellent and professional piece of work was done by the photographer Mark and his colleagues, which I know readers will also appreciate. Thank you to Cybernetics Imagination Systems Ltd, who provided the anatomy diagrams. Thanks also to Mick Sanders, for his patience, perseverance and attention to detail during the production of this publication.

Last, but by no means least, my heartfelt thanks to the woman who is most responsible for my introduction to, and training in, massage: Sister Liz. I love you and know all your students, clients and colleagues do too.

Introduction

Many readers of this book will have already experienced the benefits of receiving a 'professional' massage. All readers will have experienced the benefits and comfort of a sensitive touch. From the day we are born to the day we die, one of the most enjoyable sensations we can experience is the supportive touch of another human being.

When a child falls and runs to its mother for comfort, what does she do and say - 'There, there, let me rub it better'. When you bump your arm or leg against something, what do you instinctively do? Rub it. It is natural and provides comfort and relief from pain. We all suffer from stress or fatigue at various times and one of the remedies we will use to relieve them is to rub the part of the body that is feeling tight, tense or tired. How many of you have enjoyed a foot massage after a long day at work or walking round the shops and so on?

Massage, in essence, is a systematic therapy based on the basic, natural and instinctive idea of 'rubbing it better'. Of course therapeutic massage is more than this, and *The Very Essence of Massage* aims to give you, and your family, the tools and techniques you need in order to develop the basic rub into a home treatment that you can use to relieve many of the bodily problems we all experience at various times of our lives.

Massage is a difficult therapy to demonstrate or teach in a book, as it is very much an experiential activity. I have, therefore, included many photographs and illustrations throughout the book to help.

The benefits of massage have been known about and used for centuries, and the first chapter takes you through a brief history of the practice. As with most 'complementary' therapies, massage is no new crank remedy! Orthodox medicine is increasingly recognising its use, and many GPs now include it as part of their repertoire of treatments.

The second chapter examines some of the different forms and disciplines within massage, then the rest of the book explains in detail Holistic massage. This form of massage is closely related to aromatherapy, as it attempts to treat the 'whole person', ie body, mind and emotions, by using essential oils in the massage treatment and a particular approach to the massage session (see Chapter 4).

Before starting massage make sure you have read Chapter 3 'Contra-indications', as there are some conditions in which you should not use massage, and a few points about your own state of health that you need to check.

Chapters 6, 7 and 8 take you through the massage movements with a suggested sequence of movements over the whole body, and some additional movements that you can incorporate into the massage session to extend the benefits. Finally, Chapter 11 illustrates how to use massage for a selection of common ailments. For assistance on treatments and essential oils you will find *The Very Essence: A Guide to Aromatherapy* a useful companion to this book.

This book is intended for people to use at home, and is therefore not a textbook; however, in order to explain in more detail the parts of the body treated by massage, I have included Chapter 10 on 'Anatomy and physiology'.

Massage can be used by anyone, but there are some special considerations, techniques and movements that can be used on children, older people, during pregnancy, and for exercise. These are covered in Chapter 9.

Giving and receiving a good massage is truly one of the most enjoyable experiences you can have. There are a lot of people who still think of massage as something very questionable, offered in 'massage parlours' by unqualified, skimpily dressed young women! Needless to say, this is not the image of massage that professionals are happy to see, and bears no resemblance to what a true massage is all about. I hope this book helps you to overcome any inhibitions you may have about massage, as I believe everyone should have this experience.

A qualification in massage is obviously not necessary for someone giving a massage to a loved one, family and friends, but if you do want to know more about massage qualifications see the reference list at the end of the book or contact your local college - you may be surprised at how many are now offering massage courses and how well supported they are!

Chapter 1

A brief history of massage

We don't know where and how massage began, but we do know that it was being used therapeutically at least 5,000 years ago. As with many complementary therapies, massage is not a new invention but rather a re-discovery of an ancient treatment used for many thousands of years, and in many different cultures.

The term 'massage' is accepted to be a derivation of an Arabic expression 'Mas'h', which means 'to press softly'. It is to the East and Middle East that we must look to find the oldest evidence of the use of massage. Egyptian tomb wall-paintings dated 2000 BC show 'physicians' rubbing and manipulating the hands and feet. There are Chinese texts going back 5,000 years that describe a system of massage. Hindu priests over 4,000 years ago were writing that 'massage reduces fat, strengthens the muscles and firms the skin'. It is clear, then, that massage has a long and enduring history.

Medicine and therapies in general have developed differently in the 'East' and 'West'. The East has an unbroken tradition where new or modern medicines have only recently been accepted and incorporated into an holistic approach with practitioners who use both 'orthodox' and 'complementary' therapies together. The West has approached issues of health and medicine very differently. The 'scientific revolution', which began in the 18th century, was embraced and developed in the West and was successful in creating an attitude to health that separates mind, body and spirit - if something couldn't be proven by the 'scientific method', then it had no value!

Attitudes to the body, particularly in the English-speaking world, have also been conditioned by the Christian tradition, which has in the past seen anything to do with the 'pleasures of the flesh' as sinful and corrupting. This Middle Ages view is still exerting its influence today!

The current interest in, and acceptance of, massage and other complementary therapies is due to several factors; a dissatisfaction with the orthodox approach of a pill for all problems; a wish to return to more 'natural' lifestyles; the inability of orthodox medicine to provide solutions to many major chronic conditions; and the work of some significant individuals.

We have to go back to the ancient Greek civilisation to see where modern medicine began, with the writings of Hippocrates (considered the 'Father of Medicine') in the 4th century. He wrote, 'A physician must be experienced in many things but assuredly also in rubbing - for things that have the same names have not always the same effect, for rubbing can bind a joint that is too loose and loosen a joint that is too tight; rubbing can bind and loosen; can make flesh or cause parts to waste; hard rubbing binds, soft rubbing loosens. Much rubbing causes parts to waste, moderate rubbing makes them grow.'

This understanding of the benefits of massage was shared by the Roman physicians between the 1st and 5th centuries AD when a famous Roman physician, Galen, wrote, 'Massage eliminates the waste products of nutrition and the poisons of fatigue.' It is in the last years of the Roman Empire that the association between massage and 'the pleasures of the flesh' first became established, as Romans came to use massage as a substitute for or precursor to other activities.

During the Middle Ages records about massage largely disappear in Europe, although it continues to be a valued therapy in the East and Middle East. One of the most influential texts written during this period is the 'Canon of Avicenna'; this 11th-century Arab physician wrote that the purpose of massage was 'to disperse the effete matters found in the muscles and not expelled by exercise'.

It is not until the 19th century that we find massage again being written about and used in Europe. It is the Swede Per Henrick Ling who can be called the father of modern massage therapy. His interest in gymnastics led him to develop a system of exercise and massage he called 'movement cure', which he introduced in the Stockholm Central Institute for Gymnastics in 1813. This soon became known as Swedish massage.

The late 19th century saw a growth in demand for therapeutic massage, and in response a society of therapists was formed in order to regulate and promote the practice. In 1894 the Incorporated Society of Massage specified the required qualities of a massage practitioner: 'Health; not necessarily robust, for often very strong people lack the delicate, empathetic touch required; however, a delicate suffering person cannot expect to do much good to another suffering piece of humanity; intelligence and aptitude; for massage is not so easily done as some might imagine, especially in its adaptation to individual cases; a high moral tone must be kept at all costs, as much harm has been done by such as do not possess the requisite balance of mind.'

It was some time before massage became accepted by the medical profession, but in 1899 a massage department was opened at St George's Hospital in London by Sir William Bennett. The medicalisation of massage has been achieved with the establishment of physiotherapy as a branch of modern medicine.

I hope this brief overview of the history of massage has demonstrated that you can have confidence in the value of its therapeutic use. What follows in this book will help you to become an 'amateur' practitioner of massage, which I know will be both beneficial to you and those you massage. I do encourage you to seek out a qualified 'professional' massager who can both help you with your own health needs and support the development of your own massage skills.

Chapter 2

Types of massage

There are a few different types of massage that have their own methods, movements, strokes and history. Swedish and Holistic massage generally use the same strokes, but the medium, strength of stroke and movements are different. Shiatsu and Reflexology are based on the application of pressure to specific points of the body.

Swedish massage

All of the strokes described in Chapter 6 of this book are based on the Swedish system first developed by Henrick Ling. It is defined as 'the manipulation of soft tissue for therapeutic purposes'. The strokes used in this and Holistic massage are essentially the same, although in Swedish massage the six main strokes are more often used, ie Effleurage, Petrissage, Kneading, Hacking, Cupping and Tapotement.

The strength of stroke is usually greater in Swedish massage, with a concentration on treating physical problems rather than psychological or emotional ones. It is a particularly appropriate type of massage to use for sports/exercise, and is considered to be a more 'clinical' system.

The medium used in classic Swedish massage is talc, which allows the massager's hands to slide over the receiver, but prevents the body from slipping when pressure is applied. Effleurage, Petrissage and Kneading are easier to apply with talc than with oil.

Holistic massage

As already mentioned, this type of massage involves all the strokes used in Swedish massage but includes others that are more difficult to apply in Swedish massage. Feathering, Wringing, Pulling, Knuckling and Heeling are all strokes developed to be used in Holistic massage.

Holistic means 'whole person', and the purpose of this massage is to provide treatment to the body, mind and emotions. The atmosphere and environment in which the massage is done is an important factor in the whole process. Light, warmth, background music and essential oils are usually used to create a calm, relaxing atmosphere to please the mind and emotions.

This type of massage is particularly appropriate for psychological or emotional problems, but is beneficial in all cases where massage can be helpful. In order to achieve the same results despite the different mediums being used, some of the movements or body positions in Holistic massage are different from those of Swedish massage. For example, Effleurage of the back in Swedish massage is done from the waist of the receiver up the body and down the sides, while in order to achieve the same effect in Holistic massage this stroke is done from the head of the receiver down the back and up the sides. This book is about Holistic massage.

Shiatsu

This type of massage originated in Japan and comes from the oriental tradition of yin and yang, meridian lines and ki (life force). It has a direct relationship with acupuncture as it uses the same points on the body to balance the body's energy, but uses finger pressure (which is what Shiatsu actually means) instead of needles.

Practitioners of Shiatsu and acupuncture believe that the body is connected by lines of energy known as meridians. Each meridian is linked to organs or functions in the body and there are certain points along the meridians (known as tsubos) that can be stimulated in order to balance the ki. Applying pressure to the tsubo points (there are over 50 on the body) can therefore relieve conditions affecting parts of the body connected to that particular meridian.

No oil or other medium is used in Shiatsu; it is simply the application of pressure with various parts of the body, ie thumbs, palms, knees, elbows and fingers. The philosophy behind Shiatsu is much the same as for Holistic massage, ie the treatment of the whole person, the condition and the underlying cause at the same time.

There are no particular strokes in Shiatsu but varying degrees of pressure are used depending on the part of the body and condition, etc, although stretching movements are also a key element in any full-body Shiatsu treatment. This type of massage is benefiting from the increasing acceptance of acupuncture as a valid therapy by the medical profession, and you should be able to find a trained and qualified Shiatsu practitioner in your area.

Reflexology

We are not too sure of the origins of Reflexology, but we know that it was being used in Egypt in about 2000 BC and its similarities with acupuncture and Shiatsu would indicate that it comes from the same tradition.

Modern Reflexology began in the early 1900s when Dr W. Fitzgerald published his ideas about 'zone therapy'. This, essentially, says that there are 10 zones in the body from head to feet, and applying pressure to the termination points in the feet and hands will affect parts of the body in that zone. The points in the feet and hands are called reflex points.

Eunice Ingham, an American therapist, developed these ideas and discovered that the feet were more useful for diagnosis and treatment than the hands. An international institute was established in 1973 to continue and develop Reflexology, and today it is one of the most popular complementary therapies with many practitioners and clients.

Over the past few years Reflexology has gained a wide acceptance in the medical profession, although how and why it works is still theoretical. Logic would suggest that since the circulation and nervous systems both terminate in the feet and hands, and of course en route pass through every other part of the body, stimulating these points will obviously affect the corresponding other parts.

One of the most controversial aspects of Reflexology is some practitioners' claims to be able to diagnose conditions from 'feeling' granules or crystals in parts of the foot. Responsible practitioners should inform clients to make an appointment with their GP for a formal diagnosis.

Thumbs and fingers only are used to apply pressure over the whole surface of each foot in a Reflexology treatment session. When the therapist and client discover a reflex point that is painful, this suggests that there is something wrong with the corresponding part of the body and additional pressure is applied until the pain subsides. If pain persists after a short period the point should be left and returned to later in the treatment session. Some conditions will need several treatments until there is no longer pain when the reflex point is pressed.

Reflexology is beneficial for relaxation and stress relief, but obviously can be used for specific conditions. Practitioners need a very good understanding of the anatomy and physiology of the foot and hand as well as a complete knowledge of the various reflex points on the feet and hands.

Although not a Reflexologist, I know from my own experience of massaging clients, and receiving massage myself, that one of the most enjoyable and relaxing experiences is a good foot massage, so perhaps Reflexology has more to offer than at first it may appear.

The above therapies are not an exhaustive list, but a summary of a few of the main types of massage currently available and enjoying popularity. Whichever techniques, therapies or systems of massage you use, please ensure that you have done some reading and practice before applying them to other people. I am a qualified massager and use Swedish and Holistic techniques in my work, but I would not attempt to use any other type of therapy without first equipping myself with the necessary skills.

This book aims to equip you with sufficient skills to undertake Holistic massage at home. If you wish to practice some other form of massage therapy, some references are given at the end of the book, or look for a reputable teacher/course in your area.

Chapter 3

Contra-indications

Contra-indication simply means 'a symptom or state that makes usual treatment inadvisable'. There are times and conditions that make massage an inadvisable treatment and you should always be cautious in these cases. Some conditions may not necessarily rule out massage completely, but may mean reducing the pressure of the stroke or omitting a particular area of the body.

You should always make some enquiries about your partner's general health before giving a massage. When massage is given for the purpose of relaxation, stress relief or anxiety, it is very unlikely that someone's medical condition will disqualify them from receiving it.

It does not matter how well you know the person you are massaging - always ask. After all, how many of us tell even our partners everything? The receiver may not know that there is a problem with some part of the body, eg a rash or spot on their back. It is important, therefore, to stay attentive and ask the receiver about any unacknowledged problems you see or feel during the massage.

Both the massager and receiver will be focusing on the area of the body being massaged, and after a short period of time both will begin to sense when something does not feel right. If either person does feel this, discontinue the massage and talk about it.

Be aware of your own state of health too. Although giving a massage does not require excellent health or super-fitness, it is a physical activity and you will not be able to complete a whole body massage if you are generally unfit or not feeling well. Remember, you will be in close proximity to the receiver for a concentrated period of time and skin or respiratory infections could be easily passed from one to the other.

For a professional massager it is not always possible to cancel an appointment if you are not feeling 100 per cent. For you, at home, it is definitely not advisable to give someone a massage if you don't feel like it. If you have recently had an argument with someone, for example, you will probably not be in the best emotional state to give a massage!

What happens in a massage session is the responsibility of both people. In this sharing sense, if any of the contra-indications apply to the receiver or giver of massage, go gently or abandon the session.

A full massage is contra-indicated:

- Over areas of septic foci (spots, boils, etc), because of the danger of spreading the infection or infecting yourself. Use only a gentle massage around the area.
- On contagious or infectious skin conditions (eg ringworm, impetigo, cold sores, shingles, etc). As above, use only a gentle stroke around the affected area.
- Directly over the abdomen during pregnancy (see Chapter 9).
- When there are cardio-vascular conditions (eg thrombosis, phlebitis, angina, hypertension, etc), because of the effect of the massage movements on circulation. Reduce the pressure of the movements and omit additional movements.
- Over areas of inflammation or pain. Again massage can be performed on all other parts of the body.
- On sprains, torn muscles and ligaments. Avoid these areas, as more damage can be caused unless you are very skilled.
- On burns. Massage on burns is obviously not advised due to the extra damage caused to already damaged dermal and/or epidermal skin. Risk of infection is also increased, and it will be very painful to the receiver.
- Over recent scar tissue. Although scars may well appear to be fully healed on the surface, the subcutaneous tissue may still not be fully recovered for up to two years.
- Below varicose veins. Venal flow is stimulated by massage, and it will not help in this condition, which involves blocked or worn veins restricting the return of blood to the heart. However, opening up and stimulating venal flow above the area of varicose veins will help.

- In any case of doubt, eg unrecognised lumps and bumps.
- There are differences of opinion about the use of massage on people who have cancer; always consult your GP if you have cancer of any kind.

Although there are serious conditions in which massage is contra-indicated, it is very likely that massage is being denied to more people whose condition would benefit from treatment than could ever be harmed by it. If in doubt, consult your GP or an experienced practitioner.

Chapter 4

Preparations

A part from those occasions when someone requires a quick massage of a certain part of the body due to stress, aches, tiredness or injury, a massage is not something that should be done ad hoc. Once you have read this book, practised the movements and become fairly skilled at massage, you will find that people who know this will frequently ask you to 'just massage my neck for me' or 'I've got a spare 15 minutes - will you do a massage for me?', and so on.

Of course, if you can help by providing some immediate relief to a 'trauma', and none of the contra-indications apply, you may choose to do so. A full body massage, however, is not something you can do well without proper preparation.

First arrange the room so that it is conducive to giving a full-body massage. There should be sufficient heating to ensure that the receiver does not get cold during the massage. You may need to do this in advance so that the room can reach the necessary temperature before you begin. Check this with the receiver at the beginning and several times during the massage. Always keep covered the parts of the body not currently being massaged.

Try to arrange the massage at a time when you can be quiet and undisturbed by callers, children, and so on. If you have an answerphone make sure that it is on and the sound is turned down - if at all possible unplug the phone! However, if this causes too much anxiety then obviously don't do it. If giving a relaxing massage it is best to do it when the receiver will be able to relax, or retire afterwards.

Next prepare the massage area. Place a duvet, thick blankets, sleeping bag, chair cushions or something similar on the floor and cover with towels. You need at least two other towels to use as covers over the receiver during the massage. There needs to be plenty of space surrounding the massage area so that you can get into the correct positions around the receiver without twisting your body into uncomfortable and stressing shapes, knocking into things, tripping over or pushing into the receiver.

The second thing to think about is your clothing. Wherever you are doing the massage it is important that you feel comfortable and that your clothes do not restrict your movements. Loose-fitting clothes are therefore recommended, eg sweatshirt, leggings, track-suit, shorts, tee-shirt, etc. Always remove all jewellery, including watches and badges. Check that your hands and nails are in good condition and not likely to cause discomfort, spread infection or become infected.

Because massage involves extensive use of your hands and wrists, another part of your preparation should be to do a few quick exercises to loosen up those parts. Do the following exercises just prior to massaging and regularly during the session. **It is not advisable to do any of the following exercises if you have a muscular, circulation or skeletal condition, unless you have consulted your GP.**

- Hold you hands out in front of you, palms down and relaxed at the wrists. Shake your hands at the wrists vigorously for a few seconds. Relax for a few seconds, then repeat. Your hands and fingers should now feel tingly. What you have done is speed up the blood and lymph circulation to your hands and fingers, which should help prepare them for the efforts they will need to make doing the massage strokes.
- Leave your hands in the same position and stretch out your fingers and thumbs, trying to extend their length as much as you can. Hold for a few seconds, then relax. Repeat and relax. Your fingers should now feel a few centimetres longer than they did! This helps to stretch the extensor muscles in the fingers and wrist.
- Use the hand massage strokes on your own hands (see Chapter 8 'Full-body sequence'). This will help to exercise all the hand muscles, in particular the flexor muscles in the fingers.

Other parts of the body to prepare for massage are your back and legs. During massage you should make sure that your back is kept as straight as possible, ie keep your hips tipped slightly forward and your shoulders straight. If you are massaging on the floor, your legs, particularly your knees, are going to feel the strain after a short period. The following exercises should help to prepare these areas:

- To help loosen up the arms and shoulders and stretch the back, stand up straight with your arms by your sides and your feet about a foot apart. Gently and slowly raise both arms, keeping them straight, above your head, and stretch upwards. Keep your head facing forwards throughout. Slowly and gently lower your arms to your sides again. Repeat. Breathe out as you raise your arms and in when lowering them. This should help relieve tension in the shoulders and stretch the back upwards. Shake out your arms afterwards.
- Another back stretch exercise involves using a dining chair. Lay on the floor with your legs over the chair seat, bent at the knees. Make sure your thighs are as close as possible to the chair. Lay back with your arms by your sides. Gently raise your back and touch your knees with your hands. Relax back, then repeat.

  Remember to breathe in when relaxed and out as you raise your back.
- To stretch the calf and thigh muscles, a simple exercise is to stand on the edge of a step or stair with your feet about a foot apart and at least the front half of your feet on the step or stair. Slowly and gently lower your heels to 3 or 4 inches below the level of the step or stair. Hold for a few seconds, then raise your heels again. Keep your head up and back straight throughout. Repeat. Shake out the legs afterwards.
- Knees are best conditioned by doing a self-massage around the knee joints (see Chapter 8 'Full-body sequence').

Whatever exercises you do prior to massage, or as a regular routine, do make sure that you are not over-stretching or demanding more from your body than it can comfortably manage. Exercise, as massage, should be enjoyable and beneficial - no pain should be involved!

Now that your body is prepared you need to pay some attention to your mental and emotional state. Do you feel that you want to give this massage? Are there other things on your mind? Worries and problems making you anxious? Of course, all of us have various problems or concerns in our daily lives that can take up quite a lot of our mental and emotional energy. To perform a massage properly you need a full reserve of mental and emotional energy as well as an adequately prepared body.

One of the best ways of focusing your mind on the massage ahead and eliminating unsettling thoughts or concerns is by doing a 'Full Breath' several times. If you have ever done meditation or yoga this will be familiar to you, although there may be some slight differences.

Make sure that you are sitting comfortably with straight back and shoulders. Breathe in through your nose for a count of 6 to 8. Try to fill your whole lungs rather than just the top part (which is the way most people usually breathe). Hold your breath for another count of 6 to 8, then slowly release the breath *through your mouth*, again for a count of 6 to 8. Try to ensure that you expel all of the air from your lungs. Repeat two or three times. You may find that you become a little 'heady' or dizzy. Don't worry - the feeling will pass quickly. An increased supply of well-oxygenated blood is now flowing through your circulation system.

After doing this exercise you should feel very much more relaxed and able to focus your mind on the massage ahead. It can be very helpful to repeat the 'Full Breath' regularly throughout the massage to keep your mind focused and your body relaxed.

Having prepared yourself, it is now time to do some preparation on the receiver. Find out if the receiver has any problems or conditions that will make massage inadvisable or mean that you have to adjust the strokes in various places (see Chapter 3). Discuss with the receiver any areas of the body that are currently uncomfortable or tense, which may need added pressure. Ask what the receiver hopes to get out of the massage - help with a specific problem, relaxation or stress relief? Apart from being clear about the desired outcome, this information will also be needed if you are using essential oils as part of the massage. You will be able to choose the appropriate oil/s to suit the receiver's needs and please his or her sense of smell (see Chapter 5).

Explain what is going to happen in the massage and what you want the receiver to do, ie relax and enjoy it! Ask about a favourite piece of music that the receiver uses to relax to, and play this during the massage. Keep conversation to a minimum during the massage, but ask the receiver to let you know if the strokes are too hard, too soft or particularly enjoyable.

Remember that massage is a shared experience, and after a short period you will be able to sense how the receiver is feeling and adjust your strokes to suit.

Chapter 5

Using essential oils

*H*olistic massage usually involves the use of aromatherapy essential oils. Aromatherapy is a large subject in itself, and it is not possible to cover every aspect of it in this book, so I will present here only the basic information you need in order to use essential oils in your massage. If you want to know more about aromatherapy, please read my previous book *The Very Essence: A Guide to Aromatherapy* or see the 'Further Reading' section at the end of this book.

Aromatherapy is the use of essential oils that have been extracted from raw organic material for therapeutic purposes. Essential oils are obtained from many different sorts of plants and are the concentrated essence of the chemicals in the plant. Some oils can contain over 100 different chemical elements.

If used as directed, the essential oils presented here are perfectly safe to use at home. However, as with any treatment or therapy, if there are any contra-indications you should consult your GP, and never substitute a complementary therapy for any orthodox medication you have been prescribed. The essential oils I list later have some specific precautions noted, and there are a few general precautions that you should follow for all essential oils. Please read this section before using any essential oils in your massage treatments.

Essential oils should be purchased and stored with care. Make sure you buy a top-quality oil that is clearly marked 'pure essential oil' and has the Latin name for the plant somewhere in evidence. Oils should be purchased and stored in brown glass bottles with child-proof caps and a reliable dropper system. They are affected by light and heat, so keep them in a cool, dark place. Most oils will remain useable for up to 12 months if used and stored correctly. However, once blended with other oils, and in carriers, oils will begin to oxidise and become rancid, but will still last for up to three months if stored as above.

Oils work in two ways. First, their aroma stimulates the olfactory nerves, which are part of the limbic system in the brain - responsible for our primitive drives of sex, hunger and thirst. Also nearby is the endocrine system, which is concerned with the production and regulation of hormones.

Second, and more relevantly in massage, the oils and their chemicals are absorbed directly into the bloodstream through the skin, helping to balance the required chemicals in the body. Any excess is quickly expelled from the body through urine, perspiration, exhalation or faeces. Absorption and expulsion of oils will take different amounts of time depending on the size and condition of the person. Generally the fitter and smaller you are the quicker the oils will be absorbed and expelled.

Carrier oils

For massage you will need a carrier oil made specifically for this purpose, whether or not you are using essential oils. These are all extracted by cold-pressing, ie they are put under high pressure in their natural, raw state when first harvested to squeeze out the oil, and neither heat nor steam is used in the process.

There are several different carrier oils used for different conditions or skin types. All are suitable as a base to which you may add essential oils, but they can also be used on their own in an Holistic massage treatment. The following is not a comprehensive list but includes all the main carriers.

SWEET ALMOND
Description: A clear, pale yellow oil that is practically odourless. It contains vitamins, minerals, proteins and glucosides.

Uses: This is probably the most useful and widely available of all the carrier oils. It can be used on any skin type and will help in most skin conditions. It can be used on its own or blended with other carrier oils.

PEACH KERNEL
Description: This oil is slightly paler than Sweet Almond but its texture is a little richer. It contains vitamins and minerals.

Uses: Particularly useful for ageing, sensitive or dry skins, and can be applied as a lotion on inflamed skin. It is the carrier oil of choice for facial massage. It can be used on its own or blended with other carrier oils.

GRAPESEED AND WHEATGERM BLEND
Description: This blend of two carriers has a stronger colour than Sweet Almond with a noticeable aroma from the Wheatgerm. It contains vitamins E, A and B, minerals and protein.

Uses: This oil is easily absorbed into the skin and is a good base for blending essential oils. Suitable for all skin types, but particularly helpful in re-generating tissues and improving skin elasticity. It can be used on its own or with other carriers.

EVENING PRIMROSE BLEND
Description: A pale yellow oil that contains vitamins, minerals and gamma-linolenic acid (GLA), which helps to increase the production of prostaglandin hormones.

Uses: Excellent as a lotion for major skin conditions like psoriasis, and the best carrier to use for PMS or menopausal problems. It is also particularly useful for arthritis and rheumatism. Multiple sclerosis may be helped by Evening Primrose. Use on its own or blended with other carriers.

JOJOBA BLEND
Description: Perhaps the most useful of all carrier oils, it mimics the body's own oil and is particularly effective in massage. It has a more golden colour than other carrier oils and contains protein and minerals.

Uses: Very good for all skin types and the oil of choice for hair-care. The Jojoba blend can be used on its own and blended with other carriers.

Choose the most appropriate carrier oil for the skin type and condition being treated. In Chapter 11 'Massage Treatments' are some examples of carrier and essential oils to use for several different conditions. If your condition is not listed, use the oils recommended for a similar condition or choose the most appropriate carrier oil from the list above.

There are other carrier oils that can be used, but I have found in my practice that the above selection has been sufficient to treat all the clients I have massaged, and the choice of essential oils is far more crucial to the effectiveness of the treatment.

Dosage

This issue often causes confusion and difficulty, but there are two very simple formulas to follow:

Minimum dosage = 1 drop of essential oil for every 5 ml of carrier oil

Maximum dosage = divide by 2 the amount of carrier oil (in ml) used, and the result is the maximum number of drops of essential oil/s

These formulas are used to blend essential oils with carrier oils for massage, but are also appropriate no matter what method of absorption through the skin you are using. Some essential oils are very strong and should not, generally, be used in maximum dosage, but if you have used these oils before and know what is effective for you, listen to your body and follow its advice. The list of oils below indicates the maximum dosage recommended for each oil.

When using essential oils in a room burner, bath or compress, the dosage may be different. Please check my previous book or other literature to discover the recommended dosages in these cases.

Blending

There are two approaches to blending essential oils - aesthetic blending, where the aim is to achieve an aroma that pleases and lasts over a period of time, and therapeutic blending, which aims to achieve a pleasing blend of oils that can provide help for particular conditions regardless of length of aroma.

In aesthetic blending the 'Note' of the oils used is an important factor. This simply indicates the strength of an aroma and the length of time it will last. The aromas of 'Top Note' oils have immediate impact and will be the first to be noticed. 'Middle Note' oils are more subtle and longer-lasting with a softer, warmer aroma. 'Base Note' oils are deep and heavy with a long-lasting and powerful aroma. Any aesthetic blend should consist of 70-80 per cent Middle Note oils.

Therapeutic blends do not necessarily follow the same rules regarding the Note of the oils. It is more important that they are chosen for their therapeutic effect on the condition being treated. The aim is still to achieve a pleasing aroma - after all, who wants to use something that smells nasty? - but this can usually be done even if you ignore the Top, Middle, Base Note rules.

Having said this, you will see from the oils list that it is often possible to achieve both an aesthetically pleasing and therapeutically valid blend by careful selection of the oils you use. Since there are frequently options regarding the oils you use for most conditions, there is plenty of opportunity to experiment with different blends.

Essential oils

The following list of 37 essential oils includes those most commonly used for home treatment. There are well over 300 essential oils available, but most are not suitable for home use and many others have very limited therapeutic value.

The list includes information on the Latin name for the oil; the type of plant; the Note of the oil; the aroma of the oil; and the maximum dosage in 10 ml of carrier oil. Any precautions attached to the oil are then given, with conditions for which the oil may be helpful. For a fuller description of these oils please see *The Very Essence: A Guide to Aromatherapy*.

Bergamot (*Citrus bergamia*)

Tree   Top Note
Fresh; light; citrus   4 drops

● Don't use in sunlight or on sunbeds; may irritate some sensitive skins

Acne; Anxiety; Cold sores; Cystitis; Depression; Lack of appetite; Psoriasis; Shingles; Stress; Urinary tract infections

Black Pepper (*Piper nigrum*)

Shrub	Middle Note
Warm; sharp; spicy	4 drops

●   May irritate sensitive skins; may damage kidneys if over-used

Arthritis; Chilblains; Colds; Constipation; Flu; Indigestion; Lumbago; Muscular aches; Rheumatism

Cedarwood (*Cedrus Atlantica*)

Tree	Base Note
Soft; woody; smoky	3 drops

●   Don't use during pregnancy

Acne; Anxiety; Asthma; Bronchitis; Dandruff

Chamomile (*Anthemis nobilis*)

Herb	Middle Note
Fruity; appley; herby	5 drops

●   Avoid with heavy periods; don't use in first four months of pregnancy

Acne; Anaemia; Burns; Chickenpox; Colic; Dermatitis; Eczema; Diarrhoea; Earache; German Measles; Hyperactivity; Insomnia; Measles; Menopause; Nappy Rash; Neuralgia; Periods; PMS; Pruritis; Sciatica; Sunburn

Clary Sage (*Salvia sclarea*)

Herb	Middle/Top Note
Nutty; warm; heavy	3 drops

●   Avoid if driving, with alcohol and in pregnancy

Body odour; Depression; Fatigue; Irregular or painful periods; Low Blood Pressure; Menopause

Cypress (*Cupressus sempervirens*)
Tree   Middle Note
Woody; spicy; refreshing   5 drops

●   Avoid during pregnancy

Body odour; Broken capillaries; Chilblains; Coughs; Cramp; Dandruff; Diarrhoea; Foot odour; Haemorrhoids; Heavy periods; Nose bleed; Varicose veins

Eucalyptus (*Eucalyptus globulus*)
Tree   Top Note
Refreshing; sharp; piercing   3 drops

●   Avoid with epilepsy or diabetes

Asthma; Bronchitis; Burns; Catarrh; Cold sores; Colds; Coughs; Cuts; Diarrhoea; German measles; Grazes; Hay fever; Flu; Lice; Measles; Neuralgia; Shingles; Sinusitis; Sore throat; Tonsillitis

Fennel (*Foeniculum vulgare*)
Herb   Middle/Top Note
Aniseed; herby; spicy   3 drops

●   Avoid during pregnancy and with epilepsy; may irritate sensitive skin

Appetite problems; Bruises; Cellulite; Flatulence; Hangover; Indigestion; Nausea; Travel sickness

Frankincense (*Boswellia Carteri/thurifera*)
Tree   Base/Middle Note
Lemony; spicy; warm   5 drops

●   No precautions

Anxiety; Bronchitis; Catarrh; Coughs; Haemorrhoids; Heavy periods; Nose bleed; Palpitations; Urinary tract infections

Geranium (*Pelargonium odorantissimum/graveolens*)
Flower · Middle Note
Sweet; floral; rose-like · 5 drops

● Avoid during pregnancy and with diabetes

Cellulitis; Cuts; Dermatitis; Eczema; Fatigue; Fluid retention; Heavy periods; Immune system stimulant; Mastitis; Menopause; PMS; Psoriasis; Wounds

Ginger (*Zingiber officinalis*)
Spice · Top Note
Warm; spicy; sharp · 2 drops

● May irritate sensitive skins

Arthritis; Catarrh; Diarrhoea; Fatigue; Hernia; Muscular aches and pains; Rheumatism

Grapefruit (*Citrus paradisi*)
Fruit · Top Note
Tangy; sweet; refreshing · 3 drops

● May irritate sensitive skins; don't use in sunlight or on sunbeds

Cellulite; Depression; Fluid retention; Headaches; Indigestion; Mental fatigue; PMS; Stress

Jasmine (*Jasminum grandiflorum/officinale*)
Tree · Base Note
Heady; flowery; sweet · 2 drops

● Avoid in pregnancy

Anxiety; Childbirth; Depression; Dry skin; Frigidity; Impotence; Painful periods; Sensitive skin; Stress

Juniperberry (*Juniperus communis*)
Berries · Middle Note
Refreshing; herby; woody · 5 drops

● Avoid with kidney disease and during pregnancy

Arthritis; Cellulite; Cystitis; Foot aches; Haemorrhoids; Hangover; Hay fever; Indigestion; Irregular periods; Rheumatism; Sciatica

Lavender (*Lavendula officinalis/augustifolium*)
Shrub   Middle Note
Floral; light; woody   5 drops

- Avoid in the first four months of pregnancy

Acne; Arthritis; Asthma; Athlete's foot; Bites and Stings; Blisters; Boils; Bruises; Burns; Chickenpox; Childbirth pains; Colic; Cuts; Cystitis; Dermatitis; Eczema; Earache; Grazes; Headaches; High blood pressure; Insomnia; Mastitis; Migraine; Palpitations; Pruritus; Psoriasis; Ringworm; Sprains; Sunburn; Thrush; Varicose veins

Lemon (*Citrus limonum*)
Tree   Top Note
Fresh; strong; sharp   2 drops

- Don't use in sunlight or sunbeds; may irritate sensitive skin; avoid if diabetic

Anaemia; Bites and Stings; Broken capillaries; Calluses; Corns; Low blood pressure; Nose bleed; Poor memory; Thrush; Varicose veins; Verrucas; Warts

Lemongrass (*Cymbopogon citratus*)
Grass   Top Note
Fresh; strong; sweet   3 drops

- May irritate sensitive skins

Body odour; Foot odour; Travel sickness

Lime (*Citrus aurantifolia/medica*)
Tree   Top Note
Sharp; bright; bitter-sweet   2 drops

- Don't use in sunlight or on sunbeds; may irritate sensitive skin

Anxiety; Catarrh; Convalescence; Coughs; Depression; Lack of appetite; Mental fatigue; Sinusitis

Litsea Cubeba (*Litsea citrata*)
Tree   Top Note
Sweet; fresh; fruity   4 drops
●   May irritate sensitive skin

Acne; Depression; Oily skin

Mandarin (*Citrus Madurensis/nobilis*)
Tree   Top/Middle Note
Delicate; sweet; tangy   4 drops
●   Don't use in sunlight or on sunbeds

Anxiety; Depression; Flatulence; Indigestion; Lack of appetite; PMS

Marjoram (*Origanum marjorana*)
Herb   Middle Note
Warm; penetrating; peppery   4 drops
●   Avoid during pregnancy

Asthma; Bronchitis; Colds; Cramp; High blood pressure;
Insomnia; Lumbago; Migraine; Muscular aches; Neuralgia;
Painful periods; Rheumatism; Sprains

Melissa (*Melissa officinalis*)
Herb   Top Note
Fresh; sharp; tangy   2 drops
●   May irritate sensitive skin

Asthma; Coughs; Eczema; High blood pressure; Palpitations;
Shock

Myrrh (*Commiphora myrrha*)
Tree   Base/Middle Note
Earthy; bitter; musty   5 drops
●   Don't use during pregnancy

Athlete's foot; Catarrh; Chapped skin; Colds; Mouth ulcers; Sore
throats; Thrush; Weepy eczema

Neroli (*Citrus aurantium/vulgaris*)

| Tree | Middle/Base Note |
| Floral; bitter-sweet | 3 drops |

● No precautions

Anxiety; Diarrhoea; Dry skin; Insomnia; Palpitations; Sensitive skin; Stress

Niaouli (*Melaleuca viridiflora*)

| Tree | Top Note |
| Strong; hot; sweet | 3 drops |

● No precautions

Asthma; Bronchitis; Burns; Catarrh; Colds; Cuts; Flu; Grazes; Immune stimulant; Laryngitis; Neuralgia; Rheumatism; Sinusitis; Wounds

Orange (*Citrus aurantium/sinensis*)

| Tree | Top Note |
| Zesty; sweet; refreshing | 2 drops |

● Don't use in sunlight and on sunbeds; may irritate sensitive skin

Anxiety; Constipation; Depression; Diarrhoea; Hangover; Lethargy

Palmarosa (*Cymbopogon martini*)

| Grass | Top Note |
| Sweet; floral; rose-like | 5 drops |

● No precautions

Dry skin; Hair loss; Lack of appetite; Poor memory

Patchouli (*Pogostemon patchouli*)

| Shrub | Base Note |
| Musky; sweet; earthy | 1 drop |

● No precautions

Athlete's foot; Dandruff; Dry skin; Excess appetite; Impotence; Pruritus

Peppermint (*Mentha piperita*)

Herb   Top/Middle Note
Menthol; sharp; piercing   2 drops

● Avoid during pregnancy and when nursing babies; may irritate sensitive skin

Burns; Calluses; Corns; Flatulence; Foot aches; Headaches; Indigestion; Mental fatigue; Migraine; Nausea; Sunburn; Travel sickness

Petitgrain (*Citrus aurantium bigaradia*)

Tree   Middle/Top Note
Deep; sweet; floral   4 drops

● No precautions

Acne; Anxiety; Depression; Immune stimulant; Indigestion; Insomnia; Muscle spasm; Palpitations; Pimples; Stress

Rose (*Rosa damascena/centifolia/gallica*)

Flower   Middle/Base Note
Deep; sweet; floral   3 drops

● Avoid in early pregnancy

Broken capillaries; Constipation; Depression; Dry skin; Frigidity; Hangover; Heavy periods; Impotence; Irregular periods; Low blood pressure; Nausea; PMS; Sensitive skin; Stress

Rosemary (*Rosmarinus officinalis*)

Herb   Middle Note
Strong; herbal; refreshing   4 drops

● Avoid with high blood pressure and during pregnancy; reduce with epilepsy

Bruises; Chilblains; Constipation; Cramp; Dandruff; Excess appetite; Fatigue, physical and mental; Hair loss; Hernia; Low blood pressure; Lumbago; Mastitis; Muscular aches; Ringworm; Sprains; Tension headache; Verrucas; Warts

Rosewood (*Aniba roseaodora*)

Tree	Middle/Top Note
Floral; spicy; sweet	4 drops

● No precautions

Coughs; Cuts; Dry skin; Frigidity; Impotence; Nausea headache; Sensitive skin; Wounds

Sandalwood (*Santalum album*)

Tree	Base Note
Subtle; rich; sweet	1 drop

● No precautions

Anaemia; Bronchitis; Catarrh; Coughs; Cystitis; Impotence; Sore throat

Scots Pine (*Pinus sylvestris*)

Tree	Middle Note
Pine; fresh; resinous	4 drops

● May irritate sensitive skin

Arthritis; Bronchitis; Cystitis; Flu; Mental fatigue; Muscular aches; Laryngitis; Rheumatism; Sciatica; Sinusitis

Tea Tree (*Melaleuca alternifolia*)

Bush	Top Note
Medicinal; sanitary; pungent	2 drops

● May irritate sensitive skin

Athlete's foot; Bites; Boils; Calluses; Chickenpox; Cold sores; Corns; Cuts; Foot odour; German measles; Grazes; Lice; Measles; Ringworm; Shingles; Stings; Thrush; Verrucas; Warts

Ylang Ylang (*Cananga odorata*)

Tree	Base Note
Heavy; sweet; floral	1 drop

● May cause headache/nausea if over-used; may irritate sensitive skin; avoid on inflammatory skin conditions

Anxiety; Frigidity; High blood pressure; Hyperactivity; Impotence; Palpitations; Panic; Shock

General precautions

The following precautions should be followed when using any essential oil:

- Use only Lavender and Chamomile in one-quarter strength on babies
- For infants use Cedarwood, Mandarin, Rose and Palmarosa in one-quarter strength, and Lavender and Chamomile in half strength
- All the oils can be used on children in half strength
- If unsure about sensitive skin (particularly with children), try a skin test first, ie use the appropriate dose in 5 ml of carrier oil and massage into upper/inner arm. Wait 10 minutes, and if there is no reaction it should be safe to proceed
- Never use essential oils on the eyes - flush out with Sweet Almond if this should happen by accident. Consult a GP if pain persists
- Never take essential oils orally - if this should happen by accident, immediately contact the Accident & Emergency department of your local hospital
- If taking any medication, consult your GP before using essential oils

Use the oils individually, or blended according to preference. Using essential oils in your massage will undoubtedly increase the effectiveness of the treatment and will be very enjoyable, but it is not obligatory, and do not get confused or anxious about doing so. Experiment a little and see what you like - as long as you follow the precautions you'll be fine.

Other absorption methods

This book is about Holistic massage, and this chapter has explained how to use essential oils as part of your massage. There are of course other ways of using essential oils, directly on the body, so that they can be absorbed into the bloodstream.

Essential oils can be used in the **bath**, either on their own or better still with a specially formulated bath carrier. Don't use your favourite bubble bath at the same time, as the combination of chemicals may not be pleasant or safe. This is a very easy and enjoyable way of using essential oils and has the double benefit of absorption through the skin and inhalation of the vapour. Use up to 6 drops of most oils, but reduce for the more powerful ones.

Fragrance-free **lotions and creams** can also be used as a base for direct application of essential oils to the body. Use the same dosage as for massage and apply to the skin, rubbing until the lotion has been completely absorbed. Remember that only self-application is advised for infectious skin conditions. Creams can be used in the same way, but will usually be better for skin conditions as they are thicker and made to stay on the surface of the skin longer.

Another absorption method that is often overlooked, but has many benefits, is **compresses**. Add an appropriate number of drops of oil (see above) to a bowl of hot or cold water. Place some absorbent material on the water to pick up the oil and water, then hold it on the affected area until it reaches body temperature. Refresh and replace. Localised aches and pains are best treated by this method.

Other fragrance-free products can be used as a base for essential oils. **Cleansers, toners, moisturisers, body scrubs, toning gels, facial washes,** etc, can all be used to treat skin conditions in particular, and are used in exactly the same dosage as for massage. Some products have added **Aloe Vera,** which is rich in vitamins and minerals and is both antiseptic and anti-inflammatory; it is therefore a very good base to which you can add essential oils for difficult and chronic skin conditions like psoriasis or eczema.

All of the above methods can be used instead of massage, or better still as well as massage, to introduce essential oils into the body. Choose an appropriate method based on your lifestyle, condition and personal preference, but I would urge you to experiment with all the absorption methods and I'm sure you'll find that you get a great deal of satisfaction from them all.

Chapter 6

Massage movements

There are only a few different strokes required to complete a whole-body massage. Most of them will be familiar to you, either through experience or seeing them portrayed on film and television, etc. The strokes are all an extension and formalisation of movements we perform naturally on ourselves and our friends or relatives.

The strokes are easy to learn but will take some time and practice to perfect. Once you have read this chapter and tried out the movements, you will need to practise them regularly, on yourself or others, so that after a short time they become natural to you and you can do them without conscious thought.

Perhaps the most important element in giving a massage is the confidence with which you perform the strokes. If you feel confident about what you are doing, you will convey that confidence to the receiver, who will, in turn, trust you and therefore relax and enjoy the experience.

Strokes can be grouped under four general headings:

Relaxing
These strokes are used to begin and end each sequence of strokes in any part of a full-body or specific massage. As the name suggests, these warming and comforting strokes are used to relax the receiver, apply the oil and stimulate the circulation and skin.

There are two different strokes used in this part of the massage: **Effleurage** (or the basic stroke) and **Feathering**.

Cleansing
Cleansing strokes are deeper than Relaxing and are used to help 'clean' the muscles by squeezing out the toxins and waste products that the body produces over a period of time, and which are stored by the muscles but not used.

This helps to loosen the muscles and return them to their natural 'spongy' or 'elastic' condition. Stress, stiffness and tiredness can often be relieved by using the Relaxing and Cleansing stokes only.

These strokes are mainly used on large muscle areas like the buttocks, thighs, shoulders, etc.

There are three main strokes used for cleansing: **Kneading** (with which most people will be familiar), **Wringing** and **Pulling**.

Penetrating

As the name suggests these strokes are the deepest and aim to penetrate to the deeper muscles or apply pressure to muscle and soft tissue that has bone immediately beneath it. For some of these strokes the massager will use other parts of the hands, not just the fingers and palms.

Penetrating strokes will help to relieve muscle tension and condition the muscles, creating a better environment for local circulation.

Three main strokes are involved: **Petrissage**, **Knuckling** and **Heeling** (using the heels of the hands).

Stimulating

Everyone will be familiar with some of the stimulating strokes, as they are probably the most visually exciting and therefore usually used in films and television. These strokes are quick, percussive movements that have a stimulating effect on muscles, soft tissue, circulation and skin. They are toning strokes that 'wake up' the body's systems and prepare them for action.

Again there are three major strokes to be used here: **Hacking** (with which most people will be familiar), **Cupping** (a 'noisy' stroke that requires practice) and **Tapotement** (which is light Hacking for small muscle areas like those in the face).

The strokes should generally follow this sequence:

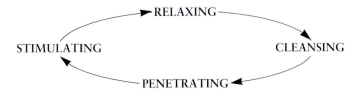

Feathering

This is one of the most enjoyable of the massage movements. It is mainly used as a gradual transition from the Effleurage movement to another movement, or when you have to break and re-establish contact with the body.

Feathering has a calming effect on the body, but also stimulates the nerve-endings in the skin and can be 'ticklish' if too light or done at length.

Keep your hands and arms relaxed and brush the receiver's skin with your fingertips, using your hands alternately. Cover a wide area with this movement to avoid over-sensitising a small area and irritating the receiver. Feathering can be used on any part of the body, but is particularly enjoyable on the back.

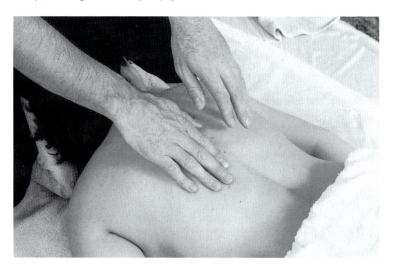

Feathering the back.

Cleansing

Kneading

One of the most fun strokes to perform, Kneading is used to squeeze large muscles or fleshy areas in order to cleanse the area of waste and toxin build-up. It is exactly like kneading dough, but using flesh instead!

Keeping your fingers fairly straight to avoid pinching, gather as much flesh into your hand as possible then squeeze the tissue between your fingers and your thumbs. Repeat the movement with your other hand over the same area. As with all strokes, keep the movements flowing and rhythmic without breaking contact with the body.

To knead an area satisfactorily the hands should be relatively dry or the flesh will slip through your fingers as you try to squeeze. It is one of the more energetic movements, requiring greater strength in the fingers, thumbs and arms to perform well, so don't overdo it!

Kneading particularly helps to stretch and relax the muscles and tissue and assists in breaking down fat.

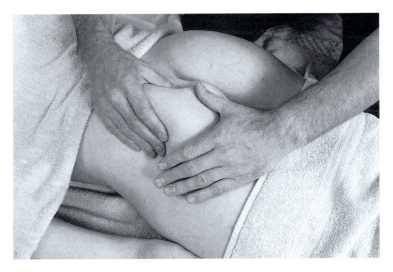

Kneading the buttocks.

Wringing

This is a useful variation of Kneading that can be done on large areas of the body, particularly the back. It has the same benefits as Kneading, but is used over areas of the body that cannot easily be Kneaded.

Both hands are used at the same time with contact being maintained throughout the movement. Put your right hand on the nearest side of the part of the body being wringed (don't massage over the spine - place your hand just the other side of the spine to begin), and your left hand on the farthest side.

Hands should be relaxed with fingers together, and the whole hand should be making contact with the body. Using a firm pressure, move your right hand to where your left hand was and at the same

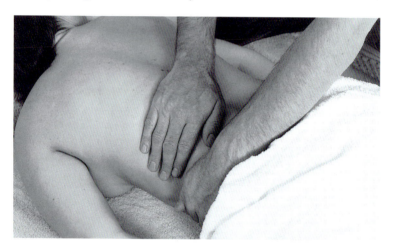

Wringing the back.

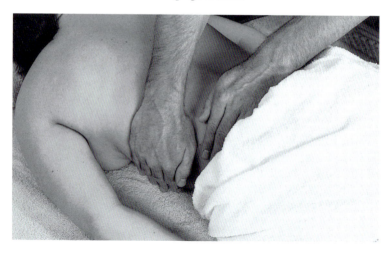

time pull your left hand back to where your right hand was, as shown in the photographs opposite.

In a continuous movement, reverse directions again, moving up the body as you do. Keep the movement flowing and equalise the pressure from both hands.

Pulling

This is not about successfully chatting someone up! It is a simple stroke that can be used on the same areas as Kneading and Wringing, and is particularly useful along the sides of the torso, the hips and over the fleshy areas of the legs.

Put one hand on the far side of the body with your fingers touching the surface of the floor or table. Use the whole hand again, making sure that you do not curl the fingers as you do the movement.

Pull your hand up and over, keeping contact all the way, with a firm pressure. When your hand can no longer comfortably remain in contact with the body, remove it. As you pull up with one hand, replace it with the other hand just slightly further up the body and repeat the movement. Work your way up the body with these alternating movements.

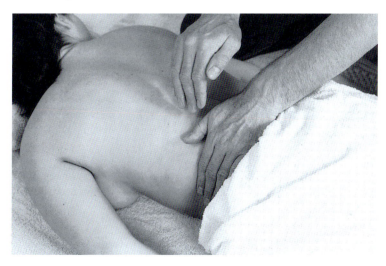

Pulling up the sides.

Penetrating

Petrissage

Together with Effleurage, this stroke is one of the most useful of all the movements and can be used on every part of the body except the face. It is a deep movement that focuses on specific small areas of the body, but it is most effective when used on parts of the body with bone immediately beneath them, eg the shoulder blades, back, legs and arms.

Petrissage will allow you to apply a considerable pressure to the deeper muscles where tension can otherwise remain untreated. It has the same effect as the Cleansing strokes but is deeper and more penetrating, and allows detailed work on small areas.

For Petrissage you use primarily the balls of the thumbs. It is important that you are not tempted to use your fingertips, as no matter how short your nails they could still cause skin tears. It may also be very painful to apply pressure with such a small area of your fingers.

Reduce the amount of oil on your hands and the receiver's body so that your thumbs do not slide ineffectively over the skin. With Petrissage you need to move the underlying tissue and muscle, not the surface of the skin. Your thumbs need to be very mobile and reasonably strong to do this stroke well.

Place your thumbs on the area to be massaged, making sure your

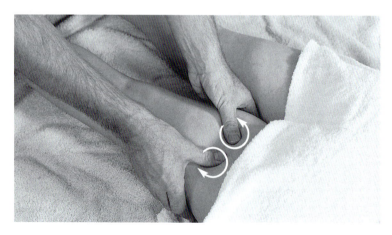

Petrissage on the back of the thigh.

hands are firmly anchored by your fingers. Your thumbs should be roughly a centimetre apart. Apply a steady grinding and rotating movement with the thumbs. Move your hands and repeat until the whole area to receive Petrissage has been covered.

It is the Petrissage stroke that will most often reveal the areas of soft tissue and muscle tension usually called 'knots'. They are reasonably easy to detect if you have a good sense of feel and some understanding of anatomy (see Chapter 10). In short, there are no small, hard muscles in the body, and if you feel a tough, lumpy area as you are doing Petrissage, it will probably be a site of muscle or tissue tension that requires some additional attention. Don't increase the pressure of your stroke, but do spend extra time on this spot to help to reduce the tension and expel the toxin build-up.

If it is more convenient or comfortable, the balls of the fingers can be used instead of the thumbs. Petrissage can be a tiring movement, particularly on the thumbs, so practice and do the exercises in Chapter 4 regularly.

Knuckling
Despite sounding like a punishment or a form of torture, Knuckling can be extremely pleasant to experience and is very effective in treating 'knots' as discussed above.

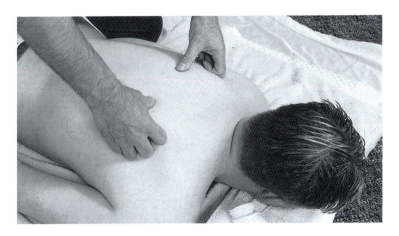

Knuckling the shoulder.

Form a loose fist with both of your hands and place them on the receiver with the middle sections of your fingers in contact with the body. Use a similar grinding and rotating movement as for Petrissage, and gradually move over the area to be massaged until it is completed.

Heeling

This stroke is a variation of Petrissage where, instead of the balls of the thumbs or fingers, the heels of the hands are used. It is useful when you need to apply a deeper pressure to a large muscle or tissue area, for example the back of the legs or buttocks.

Place the heels of the hands on the body and alternately press firmly up the body several times. When using Heeling on the back, it can be done with the heels of both hands on either side of the spine at the same time.

Your hands can either be pointing up the body so that the width of the heel of the hand is used, or pointing sideways so that the length of the heel is used - it really depends on comfort and the shape and size of the area being massaged.

Remember that this movement should always be towards the heart.

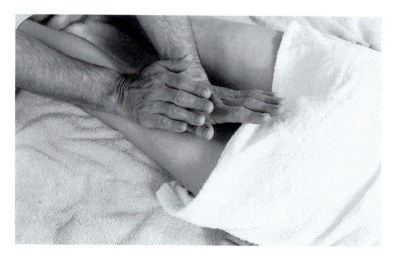

Heeling on the back of the thigh.

Stimulating

Hacking

Stimulating strokes are sometimes referred to as 'percussive' because they all involve quick, sharp, vibratory movements on the body similar to those used when playing a percussion instrument.

Hacking is a very well-known stroke, and the only one that uses the edges of the hands. It can be very effective when performed well - and very painful when not! The hands must be in a slightly relaxed condition; if they are too rigid you may end up giving the receiver a painful chop rather than stimulation!

It is helpful to break contact before Hacking, just to relax your hands; this can be achieved by shaking them briefly. Now you are ready for the stroke.

The sides of both hands are quickly and alternately used on the chosen part of the body, with the palms facing each other. The movement needs to be in the wrists, not the arms, and the hands should bounce off the body.

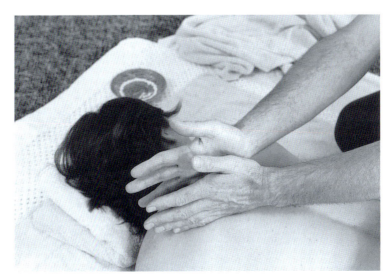

Hacking the shoulder.

At first you may find it difficult to get the hand positions correct and achieve a reasonable speed at the same time. If so, concentrate on the hand position and gradually build up the speed with which you perform the stroke.

Hacking helps to improve muscle tone, making it more elastic and responsive, and is usually used on the back, sides, neck and shoulder areas, but of course can be used on other areas. It is not recommended that you use Hacking on the front torso.

Cupping

All Stimulating strokes are quick movements that require concentration by the massager to get right. Cupping could be painful if not done well, as the stroke could easily turn into a slap! You will be able to tell the difference because the sound that Cupping makes is like a horse trotting; and the receiver will not be shouting in pain!

You need to shape your hands into a sort of cup with the finger joints straight but slightly bent where the fingers join the palm. The thumb is brought in closely to form an almost airtight cup, as shown in the accompanying photograph.

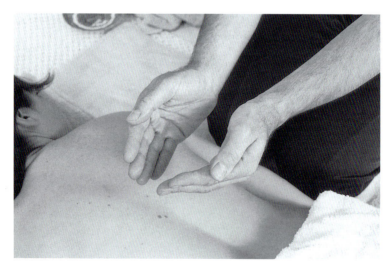

Hands in the Cupping shape.

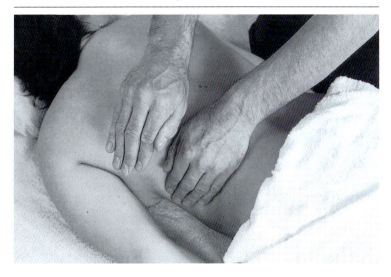

Cupping the sides.

The hands are alternately brought down on the body as quickly as you can achieve. Air is trapped in the cup and creates a mini-vacuum, which, when the hands are lifted from the body, causes a suction action. Blood is drawn towards the surface, which helps to improve the condition of the skin, nerve endings and subcutaneous tissue.

Cupping can be used on most areas of the back of the body, but is difficult to use on nearly all of the front.

Tapotement

Tapotement is the last of the main massage strokes, and is a variation of Hacking. It is particularly useful for small muscle areas of the body, like those in the face. As with all Stimulating strokes, it is a quick movement performed with the fingers.

Using almost the tips of the fingers of both hands, lightly 'drum' over the area, as if you were impatiently drumming the table, one finger at a time.

Over larger areas, like the back, Tapotement can be more effective if you keep the fingers together and bring them down on

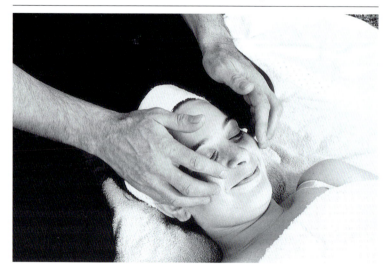

Tapotement on the face.

the body all at once. Remember that the movement should be quick and flowing.

As I've already said, it is only through practice, on yourself or others, that you will become skilled with these strokes. Some will be fairly easy to perfect, while others may be more difficult. I'm regularly told by students that the Stimulating strokes are the most difficult, although I have noted that Petrissage proves to be the stroke most often poorly performed.

You, your partner, family and friends can only benefit from your newly acquired skills, so there is no reason not to try it. Anyone can give a beneficial massage consisting only of one or two strokes, so don't worry if your hands simply won't do what you want them to! Whatever you can achieve will be more than you currently know.

Chapter 7

Additional movements

Once you have become competent and confident in using the massage strokes detailed in Chapter 6, you may wish to introduce some more complex movements that are designed to extend the benefits of a massage. These special movements can be grouped under two general headings, Body Stretches and Passive Exercises.

Body stretches

We spend most of our lives in an upright position, standing, walking, sitting, etc, and the force of gravity continually exerts a downward pressure on our bodies. You will have noted that as people get older they tend to shrink. This is not only due to weakened muscles, lack of energy and confidence. It is also due to the compression of the joints, the spine in particular, that we all experience over a lifetime feeling the effects of gravity.

Stretching the body in a variety of ways can help counteract this effect. Apart from regular stretching exercises that you can do yourself (see Chapter 4), during a massage you have the opportunity to use some stretching movements on the receiver, which will greatly help to relieve tension and extend the skeleton.

Back stretch

One of the best ways to stretch the back can be done when the receiver is lying on his or her back (use it as a first movement before treating the front of the body).

Oil your hands, then ask the receiver to raise the top half of his or her body to allow you to place both of your hands, palm up, on either side of the spine as far down the back as you can reach. Tell the receiver to relax the whole body on to your hands and arms, then slowly withdraw your hands from under the receiver's back, making sure that you keep your hands straight and relaxed as you go. Be careful not to allow your hands to stray over the spine as you do this movement.

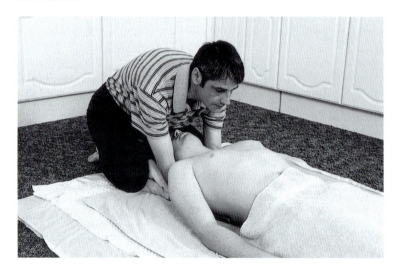

The back stretch.

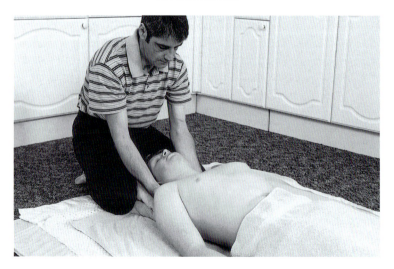

Neck stretches

There are two neck stretching movements you can use, and both can be done after using the back stretch above. The first is done by cupping the skull in both hands, just above the neck at the back, and gently stretching the neck backwards. Don't pull the neck with your hands, just gently lean backwards while still holding the neck in the same position. Hold for a few seconds, then relax.

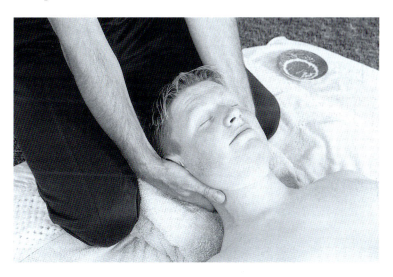

Cupping the skull for the neck stretch.

Continue by raising the head a few inches from the surface and turn it to its full extent first left then right, holding for a few seconds again on each side. Replace the head on the surface and relax.

The second neck stretch is particularly useful for the muscles surrounding the cervical vertebrae and shoulders. Move the receiver's head so that he or she is facing slightly to the left. Place your right hand on the side of the receiver's head and your left hand on the receiver's right shoulder. Gently push your hands apart and hold for a few seconds. Relax, then change position to the other side of the neck, ie your left hand on the receiver's face and right hand on receivers' left shoulder. Push gently apart, hold for a few seconds, then relax.

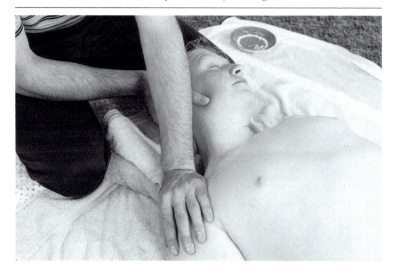

The second neck stretch.

Remember that these stretches should not cause pain or discomfort, so never push or pull the body further than is comfortable.

Leg/pelvic stretch

Having completed the normal massage treatment on each leg, you could then do a leg and pelvic stretch. While at the foot, hold the leg firmly at the ankle with one cupped hand supporting the heel and the other holding the foot. Lift the leg a few inches off the surface, then gently lean back, applying a smooth pulling pressure on the leg and hip. Hold for a few seconds, then relax and replace the leg. Effleurage the whole leg again to finish. Repeat on the other leg.

Arm/shoulder stretch

One of the main places for tension build-up and muscle knots is in the shoulders and upper back. An arm stretch can help relieve this tension very well.

Having completed the normal arm massage, move position so that you are in line with the shoulders. Hold the arm at the wrist and elbow and, as with the legs, gently lean backwards, applying a smooth stretching pressure on the arm.

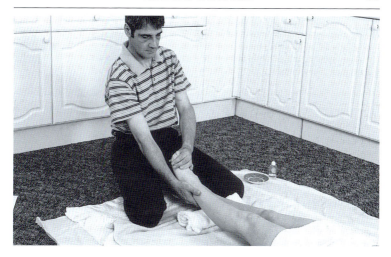

Above *The leg/pelvic stretch.*

Right *The arm/shoulder stretch.*

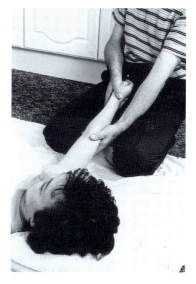

Hold for a few seconds, then relax and replace the arm by the receiver's side. Be careful not to 'pull' or 'jerk' the arm, and don't stretch it further than is comfortable for the receiver.

This completes the stretching movements that you can add to your massage session. There are a few other movements that a qualified massager may incorporate into a professional massage treatment, but they are not easily described in a book or really suitable for home use.

The one watch-word when using these movements is keep them *gentle*. Smooth movements are needed, using a gentle stretching pressure. Remember also that these are additional movements - not a requirement. If you don't feel confident about using them, don't!

Passive exercises

While the receiver is lying on the table/floor you could help the functioning of the joints by 'passively' exercising them. Passive exercise simply means that you actually move the receiver's body, without any effort from the receiver - the sort of exercise we would all probably like!

Knees

This is a very simple exercise for the knees. When the receiver is lying on his or her back you can exercise the knees after massaging the legs. Bend the leg at the knee, placing the foot on the surface. Straighten the leg again and repeat the movement three or four times.

Hips

After the knees, the hips can be exercised. From the position where the foot is flat on the surface, place one hand on the front of the hip and the other on the knee. Gently push the knee towards the hip so that the leg bends at the hip. Apply a little pressure, judging how far to go by the pressure being exerted on your hand at the hip. Hold for

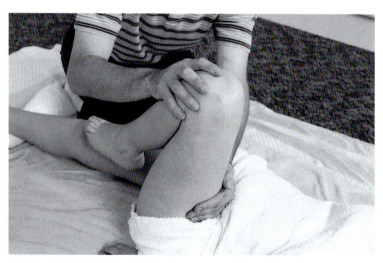

Passive exercise for the hip.

a few seconds and relax. Repeat two or three times, then replace the leg on the surface.

Ankles

With the receiver on his or her front, the ankles can be exercised after massaging the leg and foot. Bend the leg at the knee and hold it just above the ankle. With the other hand gently rotate the foot, at the ankle, five or six times clockwise, then repeat anti-clockwise. Then apply upward pressure on the top of the foot and hold for a few seconds. Relax and apply a downward pressure on the sole of the foot. Again, hold for a few seconds, then relax and replace the leg on the surface.

Wrists

After massaging the arms, the wrists can be exercised by repeating all the same movements as for the ankles.

Elbows

Simply bend the arm at the elbow and apply a little pressure. Hold for a few seconds then relax. Repeat two or three times, then replace the arm by the receiver's side.

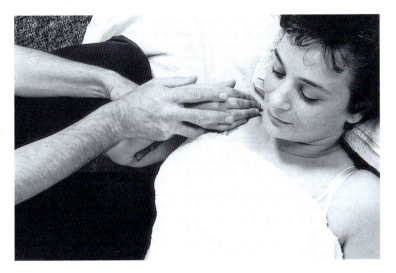

Passive exercise for the elbow.

Shoulders

Shoulders are also exercised after the arms have been massaged. Hold the arm at the wrist and elbow and move it to a position level with the shoulder. Raise the arm so that it is pointing straight up, then bring it back down to the receiver's side. Do three or four 'circular' movements, then reverse the movement and repeat three or four times.

When doing passive exercises remember *never* to push the body past the point of comfort. Watch for signs from the receiver (or listen to their moans or ouches!) that they are beginning to feel stressed, and stop when you detect them.

Passive exercises and stretching are useful additions to a general massage treatment, but must be used with care. The object is to make the receiver feel better - not cause additional pain or discomfort. Do try it if you feel confident that you can; it does greatly improve the effect of the massage.

Chapter 8

Full-body massage

A full-body massage, when performed correctly, should take between an hour and an hour and a half, depending on the size of the receiver, any particular conditions the receiver has, the need for more attention to specific areas, etc. There are no short-cuts, as this would simply be short-changing the receiver and leaving them unbalanced.

The sequence you use in a full-body massage is to a large extent up to you. It is usual to start on the back, working down the body, then the torso and the front of the body, finishing with the arms, then the face. If the receiver prefers to begin with the front of the body, you must adjust your sequence accordingly. As long as you follow a few simple rules you should be OK:

- The sequence must be physiologically sound, ie the strokes must be made towards the heart, and the central part of the body should be massaged before the extremities
- There should be as few breaks of contact with the receiver's body as possible
- There should be as few changes in your position as possible

The other important thing to remember is that, no matter which part of the body you are working on, you must follow the same order of strokes:

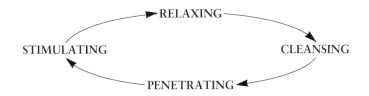

Each sequence of strokes should begin and end with Relaxing strokes. These should also be used when moving from one group of strokes to another and when breaking and making contact with the body.

Always equalise the massage, ie whatever you do with one side of the body you should do with the other. Even if you are treating the receiver for a specific condition (see Chapter 11), you should equalise the massage. Apart from not making the receiver feel 'lop-sided' it is not physiologically sound to stimulate one part of the body without doing so with the corresponding other part.

Take care to make the receiver feel comfortable. Apart from preparing the room, equipment and yourself, etc, (see Chapter 4), comfort throughout the massage should be considered.

It is not necessary for the receiver to be naked to receive a good massage. The back and torso are easier to massage if they are naked, but some women prefer to keep a bra on. This will only be a minor barrier as the back can still be massaged if the bra is undone (as long as it is not a front-opening one!). Also, very little is missed if the bra is kept on while massaging the front. Work around it if you have to - don't insist that the receiver takes it off if it makes her feel uncomfortable.

Most buttock strokes can be performed reasonably well over pants or knickers, which will allow the receiver to keep this article of clothing on if he or she wishes.

Whether or not the receiver is naked, it is important to keep covered with towels or a dressing-gown the parts of the body not being massaged. As you move around the body remember to cover areas just massaged and expose only the area you are about to massage. Not only will this protect the receiver's feelings of vulnerability and exposure, but it also keeps them warm and therefore more relaxed.

When the receiver is lying down on his or her back, check that there are no large spaces under the neck, lower back, knees or ankles. If there are, use a rolled-up towel or cushions to provide added support under these parts. When lying on his or her front, support the feet by using a rolled-up towel under the ankles so that the toes are not being stressed by supporting the weight of the foot for what will be a considerable time.

While you are massaging you have responsibility for the receiver's body, ie if you need to move a part of the body *you* should do it; always replace the part of the body you have massaged gently on the table/floor and do not leave it to drop. If the receiver has to do this it will cause muscle tension and prevent relaxation - the opposite of what you are trying to achieve!

The following detailed sequence is illustrated step by step. Use this chapter in conjunction with Chapter 11, where we apply the various parts of a full-body sequence to particular conditions.

Full-body sequence

The back

1 The receiver is lying on his or her front with the arms down by the sides and the head straight, if it is not uncomfortable. While you are massaging the back and shoulders the position of the head will not matter, but for the neck it will be important to have full access on both sides, so gently move the head into a straight position when you come to this part of the massage.

Position yourself at the head of the receiver facing down his or her back. Remember to place support under the ankles if needed, and keep the bottom half of the body covered.

Oil your hands (see Chapter 5).

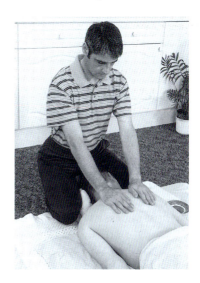

The stroke sequence:

● Begin with your hands on either side of the spine at the shoulders. Effleurage down the back with the hands on either side of the spine. When you have reached to just below the rib-cage, move your hands to the receiver's sides and Effleurage up the

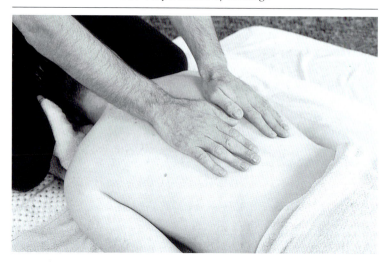

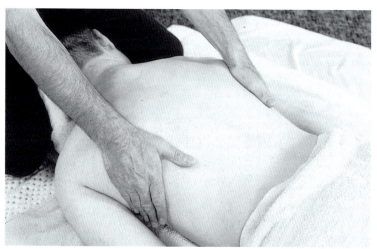

sides, under the arms and back to the start position - increase
pressure on this stroke. Repeat three or four times.
- Move your hands to the receiver's sides along the edges of both
  shoulder blades. Use Petrissage strokes with the fingers around
  the edges of the shoulder blades - change to thumbs when
  comfortable for you to do so.

- Use Petrissage strokes over the whole of both shoulder blades using the fingers.
- Use Knuckling over the whole of both shoulder blades.
- Effleurage the shoulder blades three or four times.
- Effleurage along the tops of the shoulders from the arms to the neck. Repeat three or four times.
- Petrissage from the shoulders to the neck with the thumbs until you reach the sides of the spine. Repeat.
- Use mild Petrissage with the fingers up either side of the spine from the neck up to the skull. Repeat.
- Finish from this position with Relaxing strokes over the whole back. Feather to finish.

2 There are two options for the next position. If you know each other well and it feels comfortable to do so, you can now move to a position sitting on the receiver's buttocks facing up the body.

This is an excellent position from which to massage up the back as the pressure from each hand will be equal and there is no strain on your own body. It is also the recommended position in classic massage texts and illustrations.

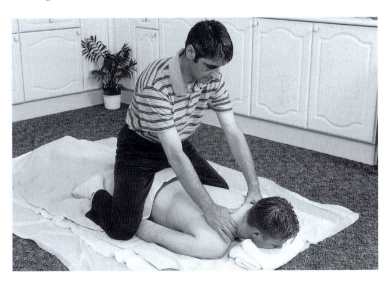

If this position is not appropriate for you, you can move to the receiver's side facing towards the head. If you are right-handed you will probably find the receiver's right side the most comfortable, and vice versa.

Oil your hands.

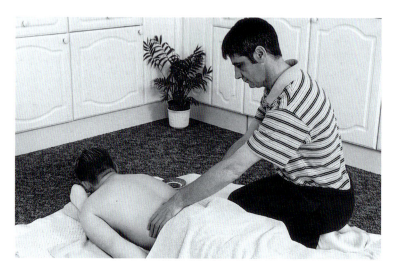

The stroke sequence:

- Effleurage up the back, with hands on either side of the spine, and continue down the sides. Repeat three or four times.
- Starting at the very base of the spine, just above the buttocks, use Petrissage strokes with thumbs on either side of the spine. Move up the spine an inch at a time until you reach the neck.
- Effleurage over the same area. Finish with your hands at the same position in which they began.
- With the hands on either side of the spine and pointing towards the head, use the heels of both hands and apply pressure in one slow, flowing movement up the sides of the spine.
- When you reach the neck move your hands to either side of the head. Placing your fingers over the shoulders and with your thumbs on the back of the shoulders, use a Kneading stroke along the shoulders towards the neck, collecting as much tissue

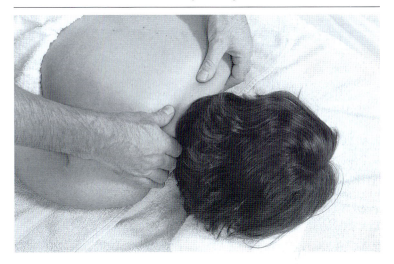

in your hands as possible and gently squeezing it between your fingers and thumbs (see the photograph above). Repeat.
- Effleurage over the area.
- Effleurage over the whole back and break contact with a Feathering stroke.

3 Move your position to face across the receiver's body. It doesn't matter which side you move to as you will be changing to the other side when you have finished this next sequence. Oil your hands.

The stroke sequence:

- Effleurage with one hand the opposite side of the receiver's body from hip to armpit.
- Beginning at the hip, use Pulling strokes all the way up the body to the armpit and back down again.
- Next use Wringing along the side over the same area.
- Effleurage again over the entire area.
- Hacking is now done over the same area. Begin at the hip and move up the side (reduce pressure over the sides of the abdomen). Continue the stroke over the shoulder blade and shoulder, where additional strength can be applied. Move back down the side.

- Effleurage the side.
- Now use the Cupping stroke over the same area that you have just Hacked. You will need to change the shape of your hand to suit the contours of the body as you move over the shoulder blade and shoulder.
- Effleurage to finish and break contact with Feathering.

4 Move down slightly to face across the receiver's buttocks. *Do not* oil your hands.

The stroke sequence:

- Effleurage all over the opposite buttock.
- Use the Pulling stroke on the hip.
- Knead over the entire buttock, including the hip.
- Use Hacking over the buttock and hip.
- Use Cupping over the buttock and hip.
- Effleurage the entire area and break contact with Feathering.

5 & 6 Move to the other side of the receiver and oil your hands. Repeat the same stroke sequence as for steps 3 and 4 on the receiver's opposite side, hip and buttock.

7 Re-position yourself at the side of the receiver's legs (either side) at the knees. This part of the full-body sequence is a little complicated with a few slight changes of position. Oil your hands.

The stroke sequence:

- Start at the back of the knee. Effleurage up the back of the thigh of the leg nearest to you. Use both hands together, one facing across the thigh and slightly above the other, which is facing across the thigh in the opposite direction (if it is the left leg your left hand should be above your right). Increase the pressure on this part of the stroke. When you reach to just below the buttock move your left hand to the outside of the leg and your right hand to the inside and stroke back down the leg to your start position at the back of the knee. Reduce the pressure on this stroke. Repeat three or four times.

8 Re-position slightly so that you are facing across the middle of the thigh.

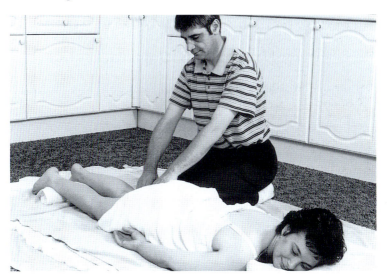

The stroke sequence:

- Knead the entire back of the thigh, applying appropriate pressure depending on the amount and tone of the muscle and tissue of the receiver.
- Wring the thigh from the back of the knee to just below the buttocks.
- Effleurage over the area and Feather to break contact.

9 Move back to position 7.

The stroke sequence:

- Effleurage up to just below the buttocks.
- Petrissage with your thumbs down the centre of the thigh to the back of the knee, then Petrissage with your fingers back up to the top of the thigh, along the outside and inside of the thigh.

- Effleurage back down to the back of the knee. Petrissage around the knee joint with the fingers. Don't apply great pressure to the area directly behind the knee as there is no underlying bone here.
- Now use the Heeling stroke up the back of the thigh from just above the knee to the top of the thigh. Use the heels of both hands alternately several times.
- Effleurage over the entire thigh.
- Gently Petrissage around the knee joint, again being careful not to apply deep pressure.
- Effleurage and Feather to break contact.

10 Move back to position 8. Move slightly further away from the receiver's leg. Don't oil your hands.

The stroke sequence:

- Now you can use Hacking over the thigh. Remember that this stroke may be too powerful for smaller people with less muscle, and should therefore be omitted.
- The next stroke is Cupping, which can be done over the entire thigh.
- Effleurage and Feather to break contact.

11 Move to the receiver's feet, facing up the body. Continue the massage on the same leg. Oil your hands.

The stroke sequence:

- Start, as usual, with Effleurage up the leg from the ankle to the knee. Use the same hand positions as for the thigh and the same weights of stroke.
- Petrissage with the thumbs from just below the knee to the ankle down the centre of the calf. Continue Petrissage up the sides of the calf with your fingers.
- If there is sufficient muscle and tissue, use Heeling up the calf (as for the thigh above).
- Gently Petrissage around the ankle joint with the thumbs as far as it is comfortable to do so.
- Effleurage to finish.

The foot

Massaging the feet and hands is another more complex sequence that I have tried to simplify as much as possible. Several photographs are included to help you.

Oil your hands and use liberally on the foot. Despite being a moist part of the body when used, the feet are fairly dry during a massage and additional oil will be needed for most people.

You'll probably need to raise the foot to get good access to the whole of the sole. When you do so, remember to give the receiver confidence by fully supporting it at all times.

Many people say that they would not be able to have their foot massaged because it would feel 'uncomfortable' or 'ticklish' and so on. Of all the parts of the body, the foot causes the most problems for most people. Of all my clients who have said this before being massaged, only one has repeated it afterwards!

Continue in position 11.

The stroke sequence:

- Effleurage the foot well, with positive contact and repeated strokes several times. Start from the balls of the toes and move over the sole to the heel, then back down the side. Use your hands alternately so that one hand can be supporting the foot under the ankle while the other is performing the stroke.
- With your fingers supporting the foot under the heel, use your thumbs to Petrissage over the heel. This is a very dense and tough muscle which will need a strong stroke.

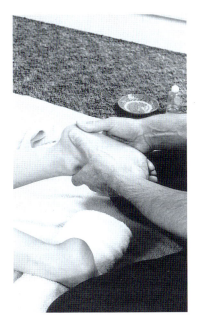

- Keeping the foot supported with your fingers, Petrissage down both sides from the heel to the balls of toes using both thumbs at the same time.

- Petrissage, using both thumbs, the balls of the toes. Start from the edges and work inwards until your thumbs meet at the centre.

- Supporting the foot with your other hand, Petrissage with the thumb of the other down the middle of the foot from the toes to the heel.

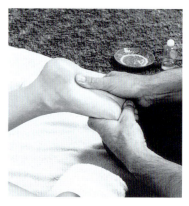

- Return your thumbs to meet at the centre of the balls of the toes. With two sweeping strokes 'spread' the foot by applying pressure with the thumbs as you move them from the middle of the toes to the sides of the foot. Move them down the foot and repeat the stroke to finish with your thumbs at either side just before the heel.

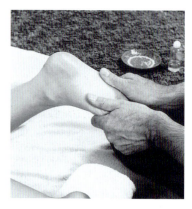

- Effleurage the foot and put it down gently.

- Re-connect the whole leg by several Effleurage strokes up the entire leg, including the foot. Feather to finish and break contact. Clean your hands before continuing (see Chapter 7, 'Additional movements').

12-16
Move to the side of the receiver's other leg and repeat steps 7 to 11.

This completes the massage of the receiver's back. One extra movement you can include, which is used to 'reconnect' the body is:

17
Move to the side of the receiver, approximately level with the lower back and facing across the receiver. Place both hands on the small of the back. With a gentle Effleurage stroke move down the receiver's left leg with one hand, at the same time moving up the back and over the right shoulder with the other hand. Bring your hands back together at the small of the back (don't break contact), then reverse - move one hand down the right leg and the other hand up the back and over the left shoulder. Bring them back together at the small of the back and rest there for a few seconds.

Allow the receiver to take his or her time, remembering to keep the body covered with towels, etc, before he or she turns over.

The front

18
The receiver is now lying on his or her back. Make sure the lower back, neck, knees and ankles are supported, if necessary, with rolled-up towels, cushions, pillows, etc.

Position yourself at the head of the receiver facing down the body, and oil your hands (see Chapter 7, 'Additional movements').

The stroke sequence:

- Effleurage down the centre of the torso, as you did with the back. This stroke will obviously need to be done with great care on women - keep one hand on top of the other going down the torso between the breasts. Continue by moving the hands to the sides and pulling up towards the start position. This is exactly the same as the first stroke on the back.
- Starting at the bottom of the ribs, use a mild 'pressing' stroke between each rib from the centre to the side ending with your fingers under the arms.

- Use Petrissage here, under both arms simultaneously. Continue Petrissage along the muscles between the shoulders and rib-cage.
- Effleurage the torso again.
- Continue to Effleurage over the shoulders and the front of the neck.
- Petrissage along the line of the clavicle (see Chapter 10) from the shoulders inwards.
- Effleurage over the area again.
- Finish with your hands cupping the receiver's head and your fingers on the back of the neck. Use mild Petrissage from the base of the neck up into the skull, making sure you do not massage over the spine. You will have to have a good feel here as you can't see what you are doing (see Chapter 7, 'Additional movements').
- Effleurage over the shoulders and the back of the neck.

19 Reposition yourself at the receiver's side. If you are left-handed move to the receiver's right side, or vice versa. Face across the body looking towards the receiver's opposite foot.

The abdominal massage movement is now done. Remember that the abdomen is a delicate area with no protecting skeleton. All massage strokes over the area should be performed in a clockwise direction, following the direction of the colon. Oil your hands.

The strokes sequence:

- Effleurage gently over the whole abdomen with both hands.
- Using one hand only, begin to apply more pressure.
- Move your hand in a circular movement over the groin, where pressure can be increased, then across to the opposite hip, pull up over the hip and side, and gently trace along the bottom of the rib-cage. Half-way across smoothly turn your hand around so that your fingers are facing towards you. Continue the movement under the ribs to the side of the receiver closest to you. Apply pressure along the side to the hip and push up over the hip, twisting your hand around so that the fingers are pointing towards the receiver's feet, and continue the stroke over the groin. Repeat the whole stroke several times.

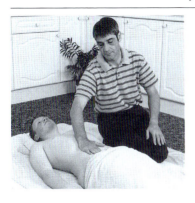 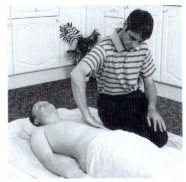

- Finish the abdomen by returning to the Effleurage stroke with which you began. Feather to break contact.

20 Move position slightly to face across the receiver's body. Oil your hands.

The stroke sequence:

- Effleurage the receiver's opposite side.
- Use the Pulling stroke along the side from the hip to under the arms and back down again.
- Finish with Effleurage and Feathering to break contact.

21 Move to the receiver's opposite side and repeat step 20.

22-26 Position yourself at the side of the receiver's legs. Repeat steps 7 to 11 on the front of the legs, but don't use the Hacking, Cupping or Heeling strokes. The foot sequence is also different for the tops of the feet. Oil your hands.

The stroke sequence:

- Supporting the foot with one hand holding the heel and ankle, Effleurage over the top of the foot with the other hand. Swap hands and repeat. Repeat three or four times.

- In order to have access to the foot you may need to rest it on your leg or raise it with additional towels, cushions, etc. Gently Petrissage down the sides of the foot until you reach the base of the toes. With the thumbs meeting at the centre of the top of the foot, just below the toes, apply a little pressure and 'spread' the foot out towards the sides. Move your hands down and repeat this stroke until you reach the ankle.

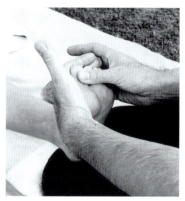

- Bring your hands back to the toes. Starting with the big toe, place one hand behind it to prevent it from being pushed back too far as you gently Petrissage up the toe from base to tip. Taking the toe between thumb and fingers, the thumb on the bottom and the fingers on the top of the toe, gently 'wring' the toe by smoothly, but fairly quickly, moving your thumb and fingers from side to side. As you do this gradually move up the toe until you break contact.
- Repeat the above on all toes.

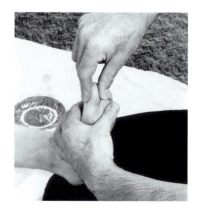

- Finish, as usual, with Effleurage (see Chapter 7, 'Additional movements').
- Clean your hands before continuing.

Repeat with the other leg.

This completes the main part of the full-body massage. You can at this point repeat the 're-connecting' stroke on the front of the body - see step 17.

27 Move back to the receiver's side ready to massage the arm. There are similarities between massaging arms and legs; as with the legs the arms are done in two sections. Oil your hands.

The stroke sequence:

- Effleurage the whole arm from the hand to the shoulder with both hands alternately. Repeat three or four times.

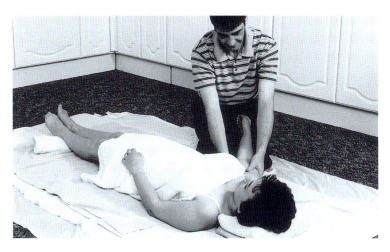

- Starting at the shoulder, Petrissage down the outside of the arm. Keep your thumbs an inch or so apart and gradually move down the centre of the outside of the arm to the elbow.
- Use mild Petrissage around the elbow joint.

- Effleurage the area just massaged.
- Turn the arm over so that the inside of the arm is now facing you. Petrissage down the centre of the inside of the arm to the elbow.
- Petrissage around the elbow joint.
- Effleurage the area just massaged.
- Turn the arm over again to reveal the outside. Petrissage down the centre of the outside of the arm from the elbow to the wrist.
- Effleurage the arm.
- Petrissage around the wrist joint.

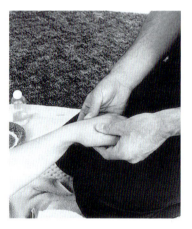

- 'Squeeze' between the finger bones from the wrist to the fingers by applying pressure with the thumb on the back of the hand and the fingers on the palm.
- With the thumbs meeting at the centre of the back of the hand, at the base of the fingers, use the 'spreading' stroke back towards the wrist and out to the sides of the hand. Do as many times as necessary to arrive back at the wrist.
- Effleurage the outside of the whole arm.

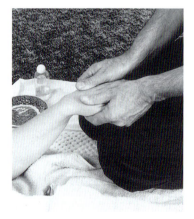

- Turn the arm over again and repeat the Petrissage stroke down the centre of the inside from the elbow to the wrist. Petrissage around the wrist joint again.
- Support the receiver's hand while using one thumb to Petrissage over the muscle at the base of the thumb. Also Petrissage the muscles down the outside edge of the hand.

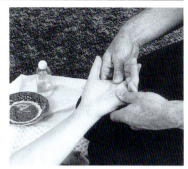

- With both thumbs, each starting at the edges of the palm, Petrissage the muscles at the base of the fingers.

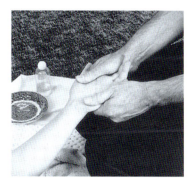

- When the thumbs meet at the centre, apply pressure with a 'spreading' stroke, taking each thumb to the edges of the palm. Repeat as many times as necessary to arrive back at the wrist.

- Place your index finger across the centre of the receiver's thumb. With your own thumb bend the receiver's thumb over until it is applying pressure to your finger. Gently press the thumb and hold for a few seconds, then release. Now use the same 'wringing' stroke on the

thumb as for the toes. With your thumb on the inside of the receivers' thumb and your fingers on the outside, smoothly and quickly vibrate your thumb and fingers from side to side, gradually moving up and off the thumb as you go.

- Repeat the above on all the fingers.
- Effleurage the whole arm and hand to finish (see Chapter 7, 'Additional movements').

28 Move to the other arm and repeat step 27 on that arm.

The face

29 Position yourself back at the original start position ready to massage the face and head. Make sure all jewellery is removed, including earrings. For the face it will probably be better to use a very light oil, eg Peach Kernel, and reduce the amount you use. No Penetrating strokes are used on the face apart from a light Petrissage on the jaw joints and temples.

If you need to raise the head for comfortable access to the face, use pillows, towels, etc, or rest the head on your knees. Oil your hands.

The stroke sequence:

- Place the palms of your hands on each side of the receiver's nose with your fingers pointing down. Use a light Effleurage stroke down the face and at the chin bring your hands back up the sides of the face to the start position. Repeat once only.

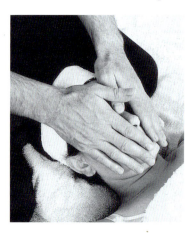
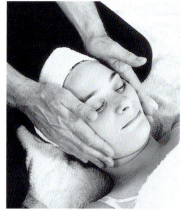

- Move your hands so that your thumbs are at the centre of the forehead just below the hairline. With a light pressure move your thumbs apart towards the sides of the face and down to the jawline. Move your thumbs back to the centre of the forehead, but about half an inch lower. Repeat the same stroke. Continue this stroke down the face, avoiding the lips, and ending with your thumbs together on the top of the chin with your fingers underneath.

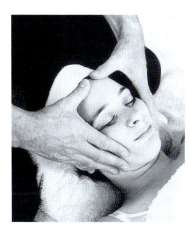
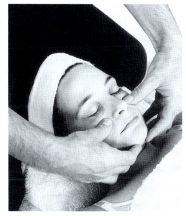

- Taking as much tissue as possible between your thumbs and fingers, gently Knead along the jawline until you reach the jaw joints.

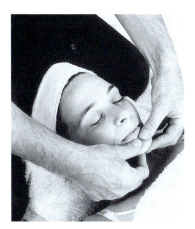
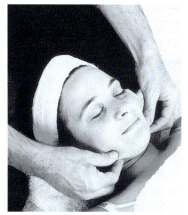

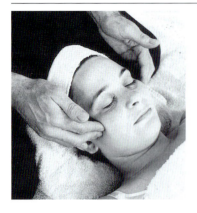 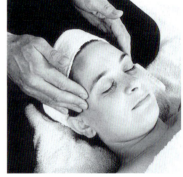

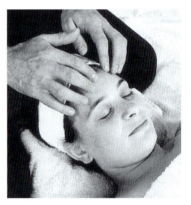

- Petrissage the jaw joints gently with your fingers.
- Move up about an inch and Petrissage gently again at the temples.
- Use Tapotement all over the face, being very careful to avoid the eyes.
- Move your thumbs to the bridge of the nose. Stroke down the nose from the bridge to the tip with your thumbs alternately several times.
- Place your palms back in the original start position, making sure that the receiver's eyes are covered by the heels of your hands. Applying a light pressure, move your hands over the cheeks towards the ears, stretching and smoothing the skin as you go. When you reach the ears hold

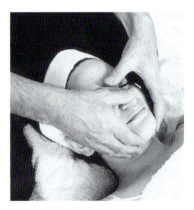

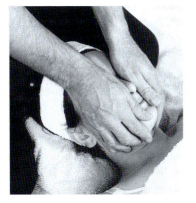

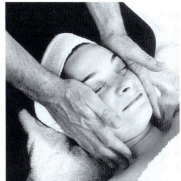

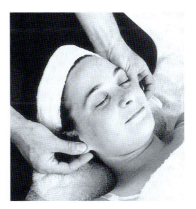

them with your thumbs in front and fingers behind, and gently stretch them away from the scalp. Squeeze along the ears with your thumbs and fingers from lobe to top.

- Finish with the starting Effleurage stroke, and end by stroking over the ears and breaking contact at the back of the head. Wipe your hands.

- The scalp can be massaged by using a Petrissage stroke all over, as if you were washing the hair. Finish by 'combing out' the hair with your fingers.

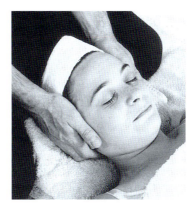

The full-body massage is now complete, and the receiver should be very relaxed and loosened up. Impress on the receiver that he or she should not jump up from the table or floor immediately. Encourage the receiver to take his or her time and gradually get up and dress. At this point the receiver may begin to feel cold, so make sure the body is covered with towels or a robe. If you have timed it right it will be possible afterwards to retire, or at least relax with a book or music.

Ask the receiver about the experience and what was enjoyable or felt uncomfortable. This will be important information for when you massage him or her again - as I'm sure will be the case.

The most important thing about massage is to enjoy it - both of you.

Chapter 9

Special massage

Massage can be used and enjoyed at any stage of life. Indeed, the sooner we start and the longer we continue, the better. If we introduce massage to our babies and children they will view it as a normal activity that they look forward to and will pass on to others.

The previous chapters have described, in detail, massage for ordinary adults in general. Although massage can be used at any stage or in any circumstances, there will be a few adjustments to make to your treatment to make it suitable for everyone. This chapter briefly describes massage in some special situations - Pregnancy, Babies and children, Exercise and Later Life. In most cases the differences are fairly obvious, eg reducing the pressure on children and older people and increasing the warmth in the room, etc.

Pregnancy

The first thing to point out about massage in pregnancy is the use of essential oils. There are some restrictions regarding the oils you should use, so please read Chapter 5 before you begin, or read more about essential oils in my previous book or others.

During the early stages of pregnancy it will usually be possible to follow the full-body sequence as described in Chapter 9. In the later months, or when the abdomen begins to swell, it will no longer be possible or safe for the woman to lie on her front. An alternative position is for her to lie on her side. In this position it will still be possible to massage the back, but it will mean adjusting your position and strokes; they will need to be done from the side rather than from the head, with the strokes pushing upwards, not pulling upwards.

Lower back and buttock strokes will be most beneficial during this period to relieve back ache and encourage the muscles in this area to relax so that the birth may be less difficult.

Massage around the abdomen and reduce the pressure of the stroke. It may be uncomfortable for her to lie on her back towards the end of the pregnancy, in which case it is best to provide pillows and cushions to prop up the back so that she is in a slightly reclined sitting position. You should still have access to the abdomen, which you can massage with a slight modification of the stroke.

Many other parts of her body may be aching or uncomfortable throughout this period. Concentrate your massage over these areas without increasing the pressure of the strokes. If Penetrating and Stimulating strokes are uncomfortable for her, simply don't do them. Remember that when massaging a pregnant woman, you are massaging two people, not just one!

Babies and children

The very best time to begin massage is with your baby, and you can begin almost from birth, starting with general light body rubbing and working up to the full body after a month. Touch is the first sense to develop, and the bonding between parents and baby can be greatly helped by regular stroking. Sleep, feeding and baby problems like colic can also be significantly helped by massage.

Babies, of course, are unlikely to be quiet and compliant receivers; they may wriggle and want to participate. You can turn the whole thing into a game with lots of communication and eye contact between the two of you. They will eventually get used to your touch and begin to relax and enjoy it.

Choose your time and be well prepared. Avoid times when the baby is hungry, tired or miserable, or massage will be associated with those feelings. Half an hour or so after feeding is generally a good time, but you will know your baby better than me. Make sure the room is warm, and that the oil is also warmed up to body heat - use Peach Kernel or similar, and if you wish to use an essential oil choose Lavender or Chamomile only, and add just one drop to 10 ml of carrier.

The best position to start massage with babies is sitting on the floor with the baby lying on your bare thighs facing you with their feet towards you. Place a towel underneath your legs in case of 'accidents'. Remember all the basic rules of massage and make sure that you have removed all jewellery and that your hands and particularly your nails are not likely to tear or catch the skin.

The following sequence can be done from a month old and continued until your child and/or you become uncomfortable with the position (see 'Children' later):

- With baby in the start position gently spread oil over the front of the whole body, but not the face. Use a gentle Effleurage (see Chapter 7).
- From the centre of the chest use both hands to move up over the shoulders, down the sides and back to the chest. Repeat.
- Move your hands down to both hips. Slide them both up to the left shoulder and back down again, then up to the right shoulder and back down again. Repeat.
- Move to the arms. Hold the baby's hand, and with your other hand loosely grasp around the wrist and gently squeeze down the arm to the shoulder. Repeat. Change hands and repeat.
- Use your thumbs and from the heel of the hand 'spread' the palm out to the sides. Hold the wrist and with your other hand gently stroke up the palm and over the fingers, unfurling them as you go. Make sure you don't push the fingers back farther than they should go - try moving your other hand up at the same time so that you have the baby's hand 'sandwiched' between yours. Repeat on the other arm and hand.
- Use two or three clockwise circular strokes around the tummy with your hand facing left to right. Change hands and repeat.
- Use the Effleurage stroke over the entire torso.
- Move to the baby's legs. Hold the ankle with one hand and with the other hand grasp around the thigh and gently squeeze down the leg to the ankle. Repeat. Change hands and repeat.
- On the baby's foot use your palm to stroke up the sole from the heel to the toes while holding the ankle with your other hand.
- Starting at the heel, use your thumbs to 'spread' the sole open to the sides.
- Stroke up the sole again and straighten the toes as you go. Use the same movement as for the hands above.

- Re-connect the front of the baby's body with both hands, starting at the tummy. Move one hand up over the shoulder and, squeezing gently, down the arm at the same time as moving the other hand down, over the thigh and squeezing gently down the leg on the opposite side. Move your hands back to the tummy and reverse.
- Turn the baby over and place along your thighs facing your knees.
- Oil the baby's back down over the buttocks to the feet.
- Starting at the base of the spine gently stroke up either side of the spine with both hands, up over the shoulders and down the sides back to the start position. Repeat.
- Gently Knead all over the baby's buttocks and stroke to finish.
- Starting at the shoulders, stroke down the back, over the buttocks and down the legs with both hands.
- Turn the baby over again to finish with the face, first making sure that you have taken most of the oil off your hands.
- With your fingers at the centre of the forehead, gently slide them to the sides of the head. Repeat.
- From either side of the nose repeat the above stroke. Repeat.
- With your thumbs, trace around the mouth, avoiding the lips, from under the nose to the chin in opposite directions. Repeat.
- Finish by stroking over the head and coming off the back of the neck.

This completes a full-body massage for a baby. You may need to adjust your movements and strokes if your baby is unhappy on his or her back or tummy. Do whatever you can at each session and progressively introduce strokes and extend the massage as your baby gets used to it and you gain confidence.

Children

As your baby grows and gets older you will have increasing problems in doing some of the strokes and in holding the child on your thighs. When it feels right to do so, progressively change the position to one where the child is lying on the floor between your legs through to the adult massage positions detailed in Chapter 9.

Adult strokes can be added as your child grows and begins to gain muscle tone, height and weight, but always be sensitive to what your child can take - each child develops at a different rate and your strokes need to be appropriate for *your* child and not prescribed age by age.

You will also know that as children grow and begin to discover other wonderful and interesting things to do, their ability to participate in a massage is going to be affected. Choosing your time is going to be critical - never force the child to have a massage or continue with a massage. You'll need to catch those few moments when they come to you looking for a cuddle or, if you've got it right, actually asking for a massage! Remember to follow the guidelines for using essential oils with children (see Chapter 5).

Exercise

Massage is well-known, used and respected in the sporting world and many athletes from footballers to marathon runners incorporate massage as part of their training routines and during an event. It is not only useful for sports people; massage will help with any strenuous or out-of-the-ordinary physical activity in which you may be engaged, from digging the garden to dancing.

Vigorous exercise increases the supply of chemicals to the muscles in order for them to work at a faster rate (see Chapter 10). If these chemicals and waste products are not efficiently washed out by an unfit circulation and lymph system they will build up in the muscles, causing aches, fatigue and cramp. Pre-exercise massage will help to condition the muscles and circulation in preparation for the exertion ahead. This will help to prevent strains, sprains, ligament injuries and muscle tears.

Pre-exercise massage can be given some time before the activity, but there shouldn't be a significant gap between massage and activity. Use the full-body sequence (Chapter 8), but increase the pace and weight of the strokes, using Cleansing, Penetrating and Stimulating strokes on those muscles that are going to be most used in the activity. Body Stretches and Passive Exercises should be included as part of the sequence (see Chapter 7) to aid supply of synovial fluid to the joints and make them more supple. Massage should not be used as a substitute for other pre-exercise conditioning routines, but as a complement to them.

After exercise, massage can be used to aid relaxation of the muscles and calming of the mind. It will also help to flush away the waste products that may have accumulated in the tissues. A first step is for the receiver to have a bath or shower (with fragrance-free soap), then to keep warm with a well-heated room and plenty of towels to cover the body. Use the full-body sequence again with special attention to those areas most stressed by the activity. Your strokes should be slower and relaxing, with extensive use of Relaxing and Cleansing strokes. Work with care around any areas that are sensitive or sore, and always consult a doctor if there appears to be an injury of any sort.

Later life

There are few differences between a massage during middle years and massage in later life. It is unfortunately true that older people generally receive less touch than at any other age. There is a tendency in Western cultures to see older people as fragile and somehow no longer human. Regular massage throughout life, including later years, will help to maintain all the body's systems and therefore be valuable in the prevention of many conditions that frequently affect people in later life, eg arthritis, rheumatism, blood pressure, depression, and so on.

A few adjustments to the full-body massage may be necessary to make the treatment comfortable for an older person. You may need extra warmth in the room and additional covers for the body. Keeping some less bulky clothing on may also help, and many older people may feel more inhibited about taking clothes off anyway. You will probably need to do a lot of talking beforehand to alleviate anxieties and apprehensions.

Lying on the floor may not be a comfortable option for older people, and a table may be suitable, but otherwise do as much of the massage as possible with the receiver sitting on a dining chair. The receiver can either sit astride the chair facing the back, or sit sideways on it. When massaging the legs you can either sit to the side, lay the receiver's legs across your knees to provide support, and massage the legs and feet from the side; or you can kneel at the feet, support the foot on your knees and massage up the leg from this position. If you remain kneeling at the feet you will need to use another chair to support the receiver's leg when you massage the foot. Whatever you do, you will have to adjust your strokes accordingly.

If there are no contra-indications, pain or discomfort it will be helpful to use some of the Passive Exercises with older people, particularly exercising the ankles and wrists. Obviously reduce the pressure of the strokes used, as the skin is less elastic and more liable to tear and the muscle quantity and tone will probably be reduced. Concentrate on Relaxing and Cleansing strokes.

Any carrier oil is suitable for older people, depending on other conditions or needs, but a lighter oil such as Peach Kernel or Grapeseed will probably be most effective.

Regardless of age, always follow the contra-indications guidelines (Chapter 3) and all should be well.

As you can see, massage is something that can be enjoyed at any age and in any circumstances. If you can establish a routine of massage with babies, it will stay with them through their lives and will be passed on to their children and so on. Although massage is an excellent therapy to aid treatment of specific conditions, it is more useful as a part of you and your family's lifestyle. Prevention is always better than cure, and a habit, good as well as bad, is difficult to break!

Chapter 10

Anatomy and physiology

As I said at the beginning, this book is not intended as a textbook to be used by serious students of massage. Its main focus is to give ordinary people enough information to be able to use massage at home with their partners, friends, relatives and so on.

When you begin it is best to concentrate on the strokes and their sequence; this will give you a good 'feel' for the body, how it is connected, which parts are soft and which parts have bone beneath, etc. Some of you, however, will want to know more about the body and how it works. As you become more skilled at giving a massage you will want to learn more about the body's systems and the effects that your strokes are having.

This chapter gives you a broad overview of the body, covering all its main systems and how they work. It is by no means comprehensive, and if you wish to know more there are plenty of other publications that can extend your knowledge. When studying to become a professional massager you will need to know more than I cover here.

There are several interrelated and interdependent systems in the body, and they all have their specific purposes in maintaining the efficient working of the whole. This chapter uses illustrations to show the size and position of most of the systems and main organs of the body, ie the anatomy, with accompanying text that briefly explains the main functions of those systems and organs and how they work, ie the physiology.

I have tried to make the text as understandable as possible and have avoided scientific or medical jargon where I can. This is, of course, unavoidable in some cases. I have also concentrated on giving information that is particularly relevant to massage, and this chapter will therefore not satisfy the needs of, for example, a medical or nursing student.

I hope that you will find what I present to you interesting and that you are stimulated to find out more about one of the most fascinating and incredible organisms on this earth - the human body.

The skeletal system

The skeleton is the framework of the body and comprises over 200 bones (slightly more in children than in adults). It has two basic functions: protecting major organs like the brain (skull), heart and lungs (rib-cage), etc, and making movement of the body possible via its system of levers (joints).

Many people think of bone as inert, dry and 'dead'. It is in fact a living organ, which is dry on the outside and moist inside. Being a living organ it requires constant nourishment. Bones are mostly made up of calcium phosphate, magnesium salts, fibrous material and water. Some bones, eg the femur, also manufacture red blood cells and some white blood cells in the marrow. Bone's hard surface surrounds the bone marrow, which in turn surrounds the artery running through the centre of the bone. The artery supplies the bone with the nutrients it needs to replace lost and dead cells.

Joints are the levers of the skeleton and are created where two or more bones join. There are different sorts of joints: fixed joints, which are not hinged and don't move, eg skull joints; limited movement joints, which require a small amount of movement, eg at the ends of the clavicle; and freely moving joints, which include all of the major joints in the body.

Freely moving joints are further classified as:

- hinge joints, like the elbow and knee (incidentally, if it was not for the patella, or kneecap, the knee would be able to move both backwards and forwards)
- ball-and-socket joints, found in the hip and shoulder
- pivot joints, where the radius and ulna (forearm bones) join, and axis joint (where the spine joins the skull)
- gliding joints, at the ankles and wrists

It is the freely moving joints that benefit most from massage. They are enclosed by fibrous material and supported by ligaments. The

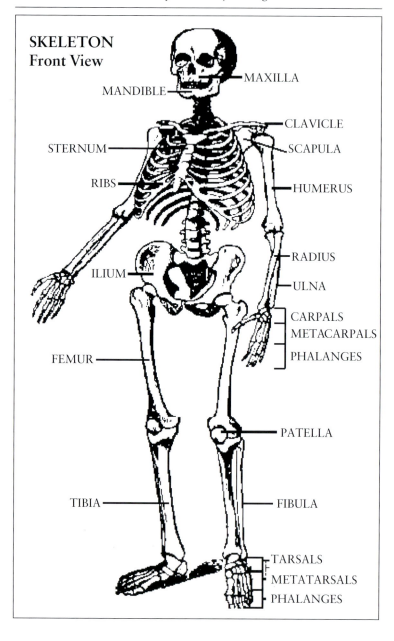

SKELETON
Front View

MANDIBLE

MAXILLA

CLAVICLE

STERNUM

SCAPULA

RIBS

HUMERUS

RADIUS

ULNA

ILIUM

CARPALS
METACARPALS
PHALANGES

FEMUR

PATELLA

TIBIA

FIBULA

TARSALS
METATARSALS
PHALANGES

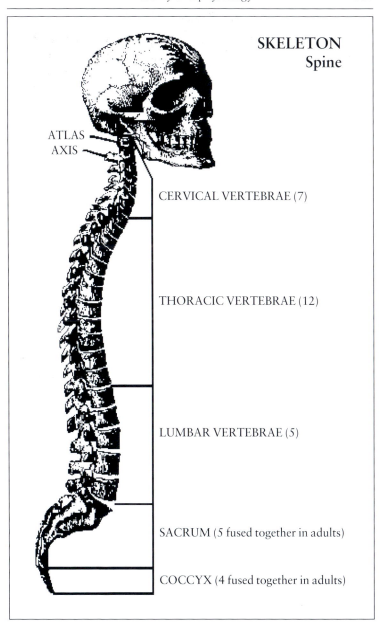

SKELETON
Spine

ATLAS

AXIS

CERVICAL VERTEBRAE (7)

THORACIC VERTEBRAE (12)

LUMBAR VERTEBRAE (5)

SACRUM (5 fused together in adults)

COCCYX (4 fused together in adults)

fibrous material is lined with a synovial membrane and the cavity is filled with synovial fluid, which looks and feels very much like raw egg-white and acts as the joints' lubricating oil. Massage around these joints encourages the production of this fluid and therefore helps to lubricate the joint, making it move more freely.

The most common skeletal problems are fractures (breaks - which can be one of five types), arthritis, of which there are many types, and spinal curvature, which can be outwards (Kyphosis), inwards (Lordosis) or sidewards (Scoliosis).

The muscular system

Approximately half our body weight is contained in our muscles. Their primary function is to enable us to move, and in order to do this they are attached, usually, to bones. There are two main types of muscle: those attached to the skeleton, which you can move voluntarily, and those that control other organs like the heart, lungs, intestines, etc, which are called involuntary muscles.

Voluntary muscles are attached to bones and joints. Most work in pairs, one moving a joint in one direction and the other in the opposite direction. When a muscle receives a message from the brain to contract, the muscle fibres bunch up, causing the muscle to swell and shorten. The bones to which the muscle are attached are drawn together, resulting in movement.

Muscles that bend joints are called flexors, and those that cause joints to straighten are called extensors. As already mentioned, muscles usually work in pairs; when you move, one will be flexing and another extending. For example, when you bend your elbow the biceps (the flexor muscle on the front of the upper arm) contracts and raises the radius. When you lower your arm the triceps (the extensor muscle on the back of the upper arm) contracts and the biceps relaxes and stretches.

Muscles are supplied with nourishment and oxygen via the arteries and the veins, which also take away the waste products of muscular activity like carbon dioxide. Muscle activity is also largely responsible for maintaining internal body heat; shivering when you are cold is a response by the muscles to try and generate more heat by rapid activity.

MUSCLES
Front View

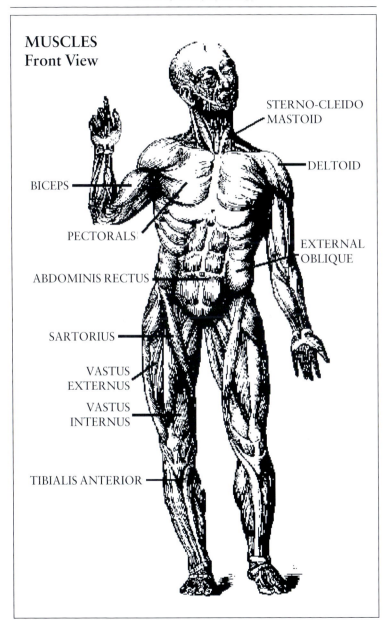

STERNO-CLEIDO MASTOID

DELTOID

BICEPS

PECTORALS

EXTERNAL OBLIQUE

ABDOMINIS RECTUS

SARTORIUS

VASTUS EXTERNUS

VASTUS INTERNUS

TIBIALIS ANTERIOR

MUSCLES
Back View

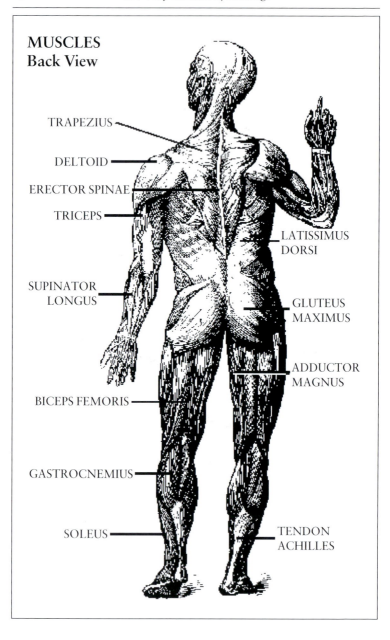

TRAPEZIUS

DELTOID

ERECTOR SPINAE

TRICEPS

LATISSIMUS DORSI

SUPINATOR LONGUS

GLUTEUS MAXIMUS

ADDUCTOR MAGNUS

BICEPS FEMORIS

GASTROCNEMIUS

SOLEUS

TENDON ACHILLES

Chemical changes in the muscle are triggered by the nerve stimulus to 'move'. The muscle will produce more chemicals and other material that it needs, and the excess is then flushed away in the venous system. Sometimes the muscles will produce more waste products than the venous system can cope with, so a waste build-up results in stiffness. Tension caused by psychological or physical trauma increases the chemical production in the muscle, with no chance to use what is produced, and again stiffness, spasm and knots can result. Massage can help to expel these stored wastes into the venous system, and thus free up the muscle to operate efficiently again.

The circulatory system

The circulatory system consists of the heart, blood vessels, lymphatic vessels, blood and lymph. Blood is pumped around the body by the heart, which transports about 10.5 pints of blood per minute when the body is at rest and up to an amazing 42 pints per minute during exercise. Adults have about 12 pints of blood, which means that blood makes a complete circulation of the body in just over a minute!

Bright red blood, which has been oxygenated by the lungs, is pumped out by the heart into the arteries, ending in small blood vessels called capillaries. Here, oxygen and nutrients from the blood are exchanged for carbon dioxide and other waste products stored throughout the body and returned via the veins, which contain the darker de-oxygenated blood, to the heart, where the blood is pumped through the lungs for purification.

Blood has four main constituents:

- Plasma, a clear liquid that is the basis of blood and contains sugar, urea, amino acids, mineral salts, enzymes, etc
- Erythrocytes, the red corpuscles that contain the oxygen to be used throughout the body and are produced in bone marrow
- Leucocytes, the white corpuscles that are responsible for fighting invading organisms
- Platelets, necessary for the coagulation of the blood.

Massage aids the venous flow to the heart, which means more efficient elimination of waste and increased oxygen in the tissues.

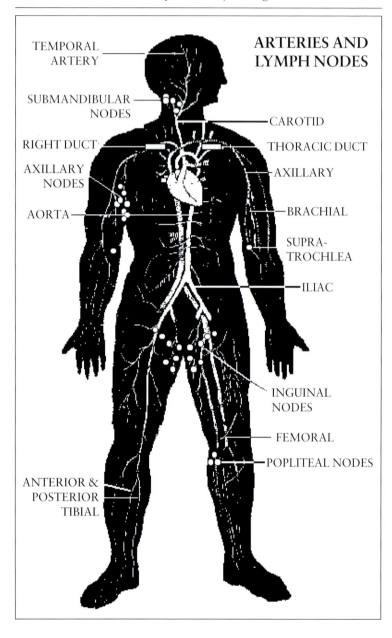

ARTERIES AND
LYMPH NODES

TEMPORAL
ARTERY

SUBMANDIBULAR
NODES

CAROTID

RIGHT DUCT

THORACIC DUCT

AXILLARY
NODES

AXILLARY

AORTA

BRACHIAL

SUPRA-
TROCHLEA

ILIAC

INGUINAL
NODES

FEMORAL

POPLITEAL NODES

ANTERIOR &
POSTERIOR
TIBIAL

The lymphatic system is a secondary circulation system that follows very closely the same route as the blood circulation. It is responsible for maintaining the correct fluid balance in the tissues and the blood, and for removing bacteria and other waste products. It contains a milky fluid called lymph, which is pumped through the lymph vessels by surrounding muscles.

The lymph is filtered by nodes or glands spread throughout the system, but there are some clusters of nodes in various parts of the body, eg submandibular (underneath the mandible) and popliteal (behind the knee). The nodes also produce the white blood cells called lymphocytes. Two ducts in the chest connect the lymphatic system with the circulation system. Massage aids the lymph flow in much the same way as it aids the venous flow.

Skin

Skin is the largest organ of the body, and has a far more complex structure than most people realise; it is, of course, a major beneficiary of massage. Its functions are as a protective covering, to regulate body temperature and to supply sensory information about the environment. The condition of your skin is a major indicator of your

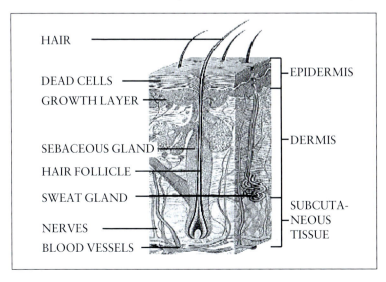

overall physical and mental health; it is the most densely populated part of the body, with over 3 million cells to every square centimetre!

The skin has two layers. The epidermis is the outer layer, which largely consists of dead skin cells (skin cells last on average for two months) and nerve endings. Although there are no blood vessels to provide nourishment, the underlying layer of skin, the dermis, provides fluid to the epidermis. The dermis is a much thicker layer, which contains hair muscles supporting the hair follicles; sebaceous glands, which secrete sebum (oil) to help the migration of cells from the dermis to the surface and the growth of hair; sweat glands, which take waste products from the body and discharge them to the skin's surface as sweat; and nerve endings, which transmit information to the brain about pain, temperature and touch.

The neurological system

The neurological system is responsible for communicating information, from external and internal sources, to the brain, which it receives from a large and complex system of nerves. In reverse, the nervous system is responsible for sending messages from the brain to every part of the body and stimulating a response of some kind.

There are two main divisions of the system. The first is called the central nervous system; this consists of the brain and the spinal cord, which communicate with all parts of the body. The second is the autonomic nervous system, which regulates all the body systems over which we have no control, ie the organs of the body. The autonomic nervous system is further divided into sympathetic and parasympathetic systems, controlling different parts of the body.

Massage can help to improve the nerve pathways, and by stimulating all the other systems massage also stimulates the nervous system.

The digestive system

The digestive system's main responsibility is to convert what we put into the body into material that can be used by the body. Starting at the mouth, the digestive system includes:

- the tongue
- the salivary glands, which are a link to the endocrine system via the pituitary gland
- the pharynx, which links the mouth, nose, ears and oesophagus
- the oesophagus, which runs from the pharynx to the stomach and is a long tube lined with mucous membranes
- the stomach, which contains the enzymes mainly responsible for breaking the food down into useable substances
- the smaller intestine, through which these substances then pass and where various components are extracted, eg fat, sugar, protein, etc
- the large intestine, which follows on from the smaller intestine, through the ascending colon (on the right), to the transverse colon running from right to left at the base of the rib-cage, then through the descending colon on the left, the sigmoid colon in the pelvic cavity, and down the rectum to the anus

Other organs involved in the digestive system include the liver, on the right-hand side just below the diaphragm. The largest organ in the body, the liver has many important functions including the detoxification of molecules to render them harmless; the manufacture and storage (in the gall bladder) of bile, which is used to digest the substances in the intestines, particularly fats; and as a blood reservoir and storage organ for vitamins and glycogen (blood sugar).

The pancreas, which is also connected to the smaller intestine at the same point as the gall bladder, is situated just below the stomach on the opposite side of the body from the liver and is mainly responsible for releasing pancreatic juices into the smaller intestine to help break down the material there. Insulin is produced in the pancreas by some specialised cells called the islets of Langerhans and fed directly into the circulation system.

Massage over the abdomen will obviously affect the workings of the stomach, intestines and so on. This is why it is important to massage in a clockwise direction, as this is the route that substances in these organs take. Digestive system problems and maintenance of an efficient system can be greatly helped by massage.

The respiratory system

The intake of oxygen and the expulsion of carbon dioxide and water are the main duties of the respiratory system. The respiratory tract is made up of several organs with the nasal cavity, throat and larynx (voice box) in the upper respiratory tract, and the trachea (windpipe), bronchi and lungs in the lower respiratory tract.

The main organs in the system are, of course, the lungs, which are in the upper part of the chest and are operated by the diaphragm, a wall of muscle running across the chest just below the lungs. When we breathe we are in fact contracting the diaphragm, which pulls down the thorax (the lungs, rib-cage and muscles from neck to abdomen), increasing its volume and decreasing the atmospheric pressure in the lungs, which causes air to rush in; then conversely relaxing the diaphragm, which pushes up the thorax, reducing the volume and air pressure and causing the air to rush out.

When the air is pulled down into the lungs, billions of minute air sacs called alveoli, which are surrounded by capillaries, transport the oxygen in the air to the blood, and take carbon dioxide from the blood, which is then expelled.

Massage of the upper and lower respiratory tracts can provide a great deal of relief to most respiratory system problems and can be particularly useful to the circulation or for tension, stress and anxiety.

The endocrine system

This is the chemical plant of the body, producing hormones that cause various changes in many different parts of the body. If we exclude the sweat glands, of which there are millions, the system consists of eight main glands:

- Lachrymal, which produces tears to lubricate the eyes and wash out any foreign bodies
- Salivary, producing saliva that lubricates the mouth and begins the digestive process

- Thyroid, glands situated in the neck that develop the sex organs
- Parathyroid, located with the Thyroid glands, which maintain the balance of calcium and phosphorous in the blood and bones
- Adrenal, which lie on top of the kidneys (on either side of the body, towards the back and just below the rib-cage), controlling sodium and potassium, storing glucose and affecting the production of sex hormones. Adrenalin is also produced; a powerful vasoconstrictor (making the veins narrow), it raises blood pressure and blood sugar, and is produced as a response to excitement, fear, anger, and so on.
- Gonads - the testes in men and ovaries in women - which produce the sex hormones oestrogen, progesterone and testosterone, responsible for the development of breasts, pubic and axillary hair, voice changes, muscle mass, etc.
- Pancreas, a part of which produces insulin, which regulates blood sugar and the conversion of sugar into heat and energy
- Pituitary, which is located in the limbic area of the brain and is in overall charge of the endocrine system, producing several different hormones to both duplicate and regulate some of the other glands' activities

All the hormones produced by the endocrine system are released directly into the blood stream and find their way to the designated organ. When hormones reach the liver it makes them inactive and passes them to the kidneys for excretion.

Using essential oils in your massage can have some impact on the hormone levels and their production in the body, which may be one of the reasons for their effectiveness.

I said at the beginning of this chapter that my aim was not to produce a textbook for massage, nursing or medical students, but to present the average person at home with some interesting information to help develop massage practice.

I hope you feel that I've judged the amount correctly, and that the detail covered is appropriate for this purpose. This chapter may be one that you will read and consult after practising the strokes and massage sequence for some time. When you do, please remember that there is much more to be discovered about the human body and how it functions. If your interest has been raised, look at the reference section at the end of this book for further reading.

Chapter 11

Massage treatments

*I*f you have read my previous book, *The Very Essence: A Guide to Aromatherapy*, you will have seen the section listing 90 common ailments with suggested treatments for each. When planning this book I re-read them and realised that some people would have difficulty in using the massage suggestions because of not feeling confident about doing massage. I therefore decided that in this book I would not only cover a basic full-body massage in detail, but would also include this chapter on specific massage treatments.

For many conditions a basic full-body massage will be satisfactory, but for others it might be too much, or not sufficient to treat the particular condition. Also, you will not always have time to give a full-body massage, and hopefully will be able to use this chapter as a quick reference to the specific problem you wish to treat.

Those of you who have not read, or do not have to hand, the earlier book, and need an easy-to-use reference to massage treatments that also lists the essential oils to use in the massage, will also find this chapter useful.

A great deal of thought went into deciding how to organise this chapter. I decided that this book should be consistent in format and true to the subject, so the following treatments are described:

- full-body treatments, eg for stress, PMS, etc
- non-specific body treatments, ie conditions that can affect different parts of the body, eg bruises, arthritis, etc
- specific treatments, eg diarrhoea, indigestion, catarrh, etc

I hope this chapter will be helpful to you and will clearly demonstrate how you can use massage for particular conditions and on specific parts of the body. I urge you to develop your massage strokes and follow the detailed instructions in the previous chapters so that you will want to expand any specific treatments into a basic full-body massage.

As always, seek medical advice if conditions persist, and if you are already on medication inform your GP.

Full-body treatments

There are many conditions that respond best to a full-body massage. At the end of this section are suggestions for general massage treatments that can be used at any time, whether there are specific conditions present or not. Used regularly these treatments will help to maintain a generally healthy body and mind. They can be used when you have a non-specific problem, just an overall feeling of not being 100 per cent.

Follow the full-body sequence in Chapter 8, using the essential oils listed below for each condition.

ANAEMIA
Inadequate oxygen-carrying haemoglobin
Essential oils: Lemon 2 drops; Chamomile 7 drops;
                    Sandalwood 1 drop
Carrier: SWEET ALMOND 30 ml
Treatment: Use regularly. Vary dosage but don't exceed 3
                    drops Lemon. Use all the strokes.

APPETITE
Over-eating
Essential oils: Fennel 4 drops; Patchouli 2 drops;
                    Rosemary 2 drops
Carrier: SWEET ALMOND 30 ml
Treatment: Use daily until appetite is in control. Then use
                    regularly. Vary dosage but don't exceed 10 drops;
                    Patchouli and Rosemary shouldn't be more than
                    10% of blend each. Use all the strokes.

FATIGUE
Physical tiredness; exhaustion

Essential oils: Geranium 2 drops; Rosemary 2 drops
Carrier: SWEET ALMOND 10 ml
Treatment: Use when needed. There are many oils that could be used, eg Marjoram, Orange, etc. Use all the strokes.

INFLUENZA
Viral infection, many symptoms

Essential oils: Tea Tree 4 drops; Lavender 2 drops; Eucalyptus 2 drops
Carrier: GRAPESEED & WHEATGERM BLEND 20 ml
Treatment: Massage daily throughout infection. Use all the strokes.

INSOMNIA
Sleep disturbance

Essential oils: Lavender 4 drops
Carrier: SWEET ALMOND 10 ml
Treatment: Massage before retiring. If a long-term problem, use nightly until sleep pattern is established. There are many other oils you could use, eg Petitgrain, Neroli, etc. Vary oil or blend to taste. Use Relaxing and Cleansing strokes only.

PMS
Pre-menstrual disturbance

Essential oils: Rose 4 drops; Geranium 4 drops; Clary Sage 2 drops
Carrier: EVENING PRIMROSE BLEND 50 ml
Treatment: Massage daily in week prior to menstruation. Most flower oils are good for PMS; use a blend that is pleasing to you. Don't use Penetrating strokes.

STRESS
Mental and emotional disturbance

Essential oils: Bergamot 1 drop; Petitgrain 3 drops; Neroli 1 drop
Carrier: SWEET ALMOND 10 ml
Treatment: Use when needed. Regular use will help to maintain
                    equilibrium. Use any of the sedative oils and blend
                    as preferred. Use all the strokes.

PALPITATIONS
Over-rapid heartbeat

Essential oils: Lavender 15 drops; Neroli 2 drops;
                    Ylang Ylang 2 drops
Carrier: SWEET ALMOND 50 ml
Treatment: Daily massage to help regulate the heart. Use the
                    same oils as recommended for stress. Use all the
                    strokes.

General massage treatments

There will be times when you do not have a particular condition or
problem to be treated, but want a massage that will help generally.
Here are three recipes to try:

IMMUNE SYSTEM STIMULANT

To stimulate the immune system and provide general good health.

Essential oils: Geranium 3 drops; Rosemary 3 drops;
                    Lavender 3 drops
Carrier: EVENING PRIMROSE BLEND 20 ml
Treatment: Use regularly with Relaxing - Cleansing -
                    Penetrating strokes. (Other suitable oils are Tea
                    Tree, Juniperberry, Bergamot, and Eucalyptus.)

INVIGORATING

A whole-body tonic to help you feel strengthened and recharged.

Essential oils: Lemongrass 2 drops; Clary Sage 4 drops;
                    Black Pepper 2 drops
Carrier: SWEET ALMOND 20 ml
Treatment: Use all the strokes: Relaxing - Cleansing -
                    Penetrating - Stimulating. (Other invigorating oils

are Eucalyptus, Niaouli, Rosemary, and all the
citrus oils.)

RELAXING

For those times when you just want to relax and calm down, eg after
a stressful day at work or at home.

Essential oils:	Palmarosa 2 drops; Marjoram 4 drops; Sandalwood 2 drops
Carrier:	SWEET ALMOND 20 ml
Treatment:	Use Relaxing - Cleansing strokes. If used after exercise (see Chapter 19), use Penetrating strokes as well. (Other oils you could use are Cedarwood, Chamomile, Lavender, Neroli, Ylang Ylang, and Patchouli. There are many sedative oils.)

Non-specific treatments

There are several conditions that can arise in various parts of the
body that are not specific to one particular part. Some may be more
common in particular parts, and I have used these common sites of
complaint in the following descriptions. Modify the treatment to
suit the part of the body affected.

ARTHRITIS
Pain, inflammation and stiffness of the joints

Essential oils:	Ginger 2 drops; Lavender 6 drops; Juniperberry 2 drops
Carrier:	JOJOBA BLEND 20 ml
Treatment:	*Don't massage if joints are inflamed or painful.* Use massage regularly between attacks. Always massage around the joints where the arthritis is sited, not over them. A full-body massage will help to reduce the possibility of other joints being affected. Use Relaxing - Cleansing - Penetrating strokes, but reduce the pressure on the Penetrating strokes. Advise the patient of additional treatments, eg diet changes (red meats, tea, coffee and alcohol have been found to be unhelpful) and stress reduction.

BRUISES
Blood seeping into tissues

Essential oils: Rosemary 2 drops; Lavender 2 drops
Carrier: SWEET ALMOND 10 ml
Treatment: Massage when bruise begins to yellow. Use local
                     Relaxing - Cleansing strokes only to stimulate
                     circulation and relieve pain.

CELLULITE
Build-up of fluid and waste in fat

Essential oils: Grapefruit 1 drop; Fennel 1 drop;
                     Juniperberry 3 drops
Carrier: PEACH KERNEL 10ml
Treatment: Massage regularly using the above. All the strokes
                     should be used and pressure added to sites of cellulite.

DERMATITIS/ECZEMA
Itchy inflammation of the skin

Essential oils: Chamomile 4 drops; Lavender 4 drops;
                     Geranium 4 drops
Carrier: GRAPESEED & WHEATGERM BLEND 15 ml
                     and EVENING PRIMROSE BLEND 15 ml
Treatment: Massage the affected area with the above blend.
                     Use Relaxing - Cleansing - Penetrating strokes,
                     reducing the pressure on Penetrating during
                     attacks. Massage daily when the condition is
                     bad, and regularly, using all the strokes, at other
                     times.

MUSCLE ACHES
General aches and pains

Essential oils: Ginger 2 drops; Rosemary 4 drops;
                     Marjoram 4 drops
Carrier: SWEET ALMOND 20 ml
Treatment: Massage daily until aches or pains are relieved. Treat
                     regularly for a short period afterwards to prevent
                     relapse. Use Relaxing - Cleansing strokes during the
                     period of pain, and all the strokes afterwards.

RHEUMATISM
Diseased muscles become inflamed, swollen and painful

Essential oils: Ginger 2 drops; Juniperberry 8 drops;
                      Marjoram 2 drops
Carrier: SWEET ALMOND 20 ml
Treatment: Massage affected areas daily until pain relieved.
                      Treat regularly afterwards. Use Relaxing - Cleansing
                      strokes during attacks and all the strokes afterwards.

VARICOSE VEINS
Damaged and worn veins

Essential oils: Cypress 5 drops; Lavender 4 drops; Lemon 1 drop
Carrier: SWEET ALMOND 30 ml
Treatment: Treatment will have to be regular and often, so vary the
                      dosage and oils. Substitute Geranium or Rosemary for
                      Cypress or Lavender. Use the above blend in regular
                      massage using Relaxing - Cleansing strokes *above* the
                      affected area - *never massage below varicose veins.*
                      Additionally, if varicosity is in the legs rest with the legs
                      higher than the rest of the body. Alternate cold and hot
                      compress or water spray treatments can help. Add some
                      stretching movements to the massage (see Chapter 7).

Specific treatments

This section will explain how to massage for specific complaints. You
will see that conditions have been grouped according to the part of
the body being massaged, and are alphabetical within each section.

Head:

CATARRH
Blocked, damaged or infected nasal passages

Essential oils: Eucalyptus 3 drops (Alternatively use Frankincense
                      or Sandalwood in the same dosage)
Carrier: PEACH KERNEL 10 ml
Treatment: Use mild Petrissage on the sinuses (above the eyes and
                      each side of the nose) twice daily until condition clears.

DANDRUFF
Dead skin cells on the scalp

Essential oils: Cedarwood 5 drops
Carrier: JOJOBA BLEND 15 ml
Treatment: Massage the scalp using mild Petrissage all over. Cypress or Rosemary can be used as an alternative to Cedarwood or added to the final rinse after shampooing. Treat daily until cleared up.

EARACHE
Primary or secondary infection of part of the ear

Essential oils: Chamomile 1 drop; Lavender 1 drop
Carrier: PEACH KERNEL 5 ml
Treatment: Using Petrissage, gently massage around, *but not in*, the ear. If symptoms persist for longer than two days, seek medical advice.

BLOOD PRESSURE (HIGH)
Hypertension; over-worked heart

Essential oils: Lavender 2 drops; Marjoram 6 drops; Ylang Ylang 2 drops
Carrier: EVENING PRIMROSE 5 ml; SWEET ALMOND 15 ml
Treatment: Treat daily until condition improves, then treat twice weekly. Use Relaxing strokes on back and chest.

BLOOD PRESSURE (LOW)
Hypotension; insufficient blood pumped by heart

Essential oils: Lemon 1 drop; Clary Sage 4 drops; Rosemary 4 drops
Carrier: SWEET ALMOND 20 ml
Treatment: As above for High Blood Pressure, but include all the strokes in the massage.

HEADACHES (TENSION)
Strain on the muscular tissues or blood vessels in the head or neck
Essential oils: Lavender 1 drop; Peppermint 1 drop
Carrier: PEACH KERNEL 5 ml
Treatment: Relaxing and mild Penetrating strokes on the forehead, temples and neck. Use only your fingers to Petrissage gently the temples. Use your thumbs and fingers to Petrissage gently the forehead. The neck can be massaged by gently pressing with the fingers from the base up each side of the spine to the point where the neck joins the skull. Lavender can be used neat on the forehead and temples. One 10-minute treatment is all that should be needed. Don't overdo it or you may make the headache worse.

NAUSEA
Tension plus feelings of nausea or actual vomiting
Essential oils: Lavender 1 drop; Peppermint 1 drop
Carrier: PEACH KERNEL 5 ml
Essential oils: Rosewood 1 drop; Peppermint 1 drop
Carrier: SWEET ALMOND 5 ml
Treatment: Treat the head as above for Tension Headache. Use the Rosewood and Peppermint blend to massage gently the abdomen using the usual strokes.

MIGRAINE
Severe headache caused by restricted blood supply in cerebral arteries
Essential oils: Lavender 1 drop; Peppermint 1 drop
Carrier: PEACH KERNEL 5 ml
Treatment: Don't massage once an attack has developed. When you first suspect that a migraine is developing use the massage as for Tension Headache above. A cold compress using 2 drops of Lavender can be placed on the forehead after massage. Marjoram to help blood supply can be used in a warm compress on the back of the neck; use 2 drops.

Back and chest:

ANXIETY
A worried or troubled state of mind

Essential oils: Bergamot 4 drops (Many other oils could be used, eg Neroli, Cedarwood, Lavender, etc)
Carrier: SWEET ALMOND 10 ml
Treatment: Massage the upper back and shoulders first, then the chest. For women avoid the breasts. Use Relaxing - Cleansing - Penetrating strokes on the back and Relaxing strokes only on the chest. Treat daily for as long as the condition remains.

BLOOD PRESSURE (HIGH)
Over-worked heart

Essential oils: Lavender 2 drops; Marjoram 6 drops; Ylang Ylang 2 drops
Carrier: EVENING PRIMROSE BLEND 20 ml
Treatment: Massage areas as above. Use Relaxing and Cleansing strokes only on the upper back, and Relaxing only on the chest. Treat daily until condition improves, then reduce treatment to twice weekly. Diet and lifestyle changes are also needed.

BLOOD PRESSURE (LOW)
Insufficient blood pumped by heart

Essential oils: Clary Sage 4 drops; Rosemary 3 drops; Lemon 1 drop
Carrier: SWEET ALMOND 20 ml
Treatment: Massage areas as above. Use all the strokes on the back and Relaxing strokes only on the chest. If condition is severe, increase Lemon and/or Rosemary *but do not exceed 10 drops* of essential oils. Cardio-vascular exercise, eg walking, will also help.

BRONCHITIS
Inflammation of the main air passages of the lungs (bronchi)

Essential oils: Cedarwood; Eucalyptus; Sandalwood (Any of the 'wood' oils can be used; maximum 9 drops of a single oil or blend)

Carrier: SWEET ALMOND 20 ml

Treatment: Massage over the upper back first with Relaxing - Cleansing - Penetrating strokes; then massage the chest with Relaxing strokes only. Treat twice daily while condition exists and weekly thereafter for several weeks. Rest and warmth are also needed.

Lower back:

LUMBAGO
Pain in the lumbar region of the back

Essential oils: Marjoram 4 drops; Rosemary 4 drops; Black Pepper 2 drops (Or Ginger 2 drops)

Carrier: SWEET ALMOND 20 ml

Treatment: Treat twice daily with Relaxing and mild Penetrating strokes over the area. Remember to avoid the spine and don't use Penetrating strokes over areas of pain. Rest the back while painful.

Abdomen:

CONSTIPATION
Compacted waste causing irregular bowel movements

Essential oils: Orange 1 drop; Fennel 1 drop; Rosemary 3 drops

Carrier: SWEET ALMOND 10 ml

Treatment: Use only clockwise circular movements around the abdomen (see Chapter 8). Use strong Effleurage covering the whole abdomen. Treat twice daily until the condition eases. Drink plenty of water and reduce fats, sugars and starches in diet. Gentle cardio-vascular and stretching exercise will also help. Constipation may be the result of underlying Stress or Anxiety; if so, treat additionally for these conditions regularly.

DIARRHOEA
Excessively frequent and loose evacuation of the bowels

Essential oils: Cypress 3 drops; Chamomile 2 drops (Any anti spasmodic oil will help, eg Lavender, Mandarin, Orange, etc)

Carrier: SWEET ALMOND 10 ml

Treatment: Use gentle Relaxing massage strokes around the abdomen as above. A warm compress on the abdomen using the same oils will also help. Drink plenty of water to avoid dehydration.

FLATULENCE
Expulsion of gas from the digestive system

Essential oils: Fennel; Orange; Peppermint (Use carminative oils like Frankincense, Juniperberry, Lemongrass, etc, singly or blended up to a maximum of 4 drops)

Carrier: SWEET ALMOND 10 ml

Treatment: Use gentle Relaxing strokes around the abdomen. The condition should respond immediately to treatment.

INDIGESTION
General sense of discomfort in the abdomen

Essential oils: As above

Carrier: SWEET ALMOND 10 ml

Treatment: As above.

Lower back and abdomen:

CHILDBIRTH
Pain during labour

Essential oils: Jasmine 2 drops; Lavender 2 drops

Carrier: PEACH KERNEL 10 ml

Treatment: Used singly or together, Jasmine and Lavender are the best oils to use. Massage the lower back using Relaxing - Penetrating (mild) strokes, then use Relaxing abdomen strokes (see Chapter 9) as for Flatulence, etc. Receiver should be lying on her side or sitting upright for the lower back strokes, and on her back for the abdomen strokes.

Use throughout birth and afterwards. Use prior to birth after first *4 months* of pregnancy.

HERNIA
Bulge of soft tissue protruding through a muscle wall (usually abdomen)

Essential oils: Ginger 2 drops; Lavender 2 drops; Rosemary 1 drop
Carrier: SWEET ALMOND 10 ml
Treatment: Massage the lower back with Relaxing - Penetrating strokes. Abdomen should be massaged as usual. If it is not painful, gentle pressure can be applied to and around the hernia to encourage it back into place. Hernias can also occur in other parts of the body, eg the groin. Use the same strokes on these areas.

PERIODS (HEAVY)
Prolonged periods with excessive bleeding

Essential oils: Cypress 6 drops; Geranium 6 drops; Rose 1 drop (*Do not use Chamomile, Clary Sage, Fennel, Juniperberry, Lavender, Marjoram or Rosemary*)
Carrier: EVENING PRIMROSE BLEND 30 ml

PERIODS (IRREGULAR)
Scanty and infrequent periods

Essential oils: Chamomile 6 drops; Clary Sage 6 drops; Rose 1 drop
Carrier: EVENING PRIMROSE BLEND 30 ml

PERIODS (PAINFUL)
Dull pain during periods

Essential oils: Marjoram 6 drops; Chamomile 6 drops; Clary Sage 1 drop
Carrier: SWEET ALMOND 30 ml
Treatment: Depending on the severity of the symptoms, massage the lower back and abdomen as for Childbirth. Treatments should begin in the week before the period is due and continue throughout the period. Twice daily is recommended, but do as regularly as possible.

NB Although Rose is classified as an Emmenagogue (encourages bleeding), its action is more regulating than encouraging.

Legs:

CHILBLAINS
Constriction of surface blood vessels
Essential oils: Cypress 2 drops; Rosemary 3 drops
Carrier: SWEET ALMOND 10 ml
Treatment: Massage the affected area regularly to improve circulation. Use all the strokes. For immediate relief add 2 drops of Black Pepper and 5 ml of carrier, and massage the area vigorously using all the strokes.

CRAMP
Muscle spasm
Essential oils: Cypress 1 drop; Marjoram 3 drops; Rosemary 1 drop
Carrier: SWEET ALMOND 10 ml
Treatment: Massage vigorously, using all the strokes. Heat and movement will also help to relieve the pain and relax the muscle. Treat regularly to prevent cramp recurring. Follow the treatment if cramp occurs in other areas, apart from the stomach. Stomach cramps can be best treated with a very warm compress using 2 or 3 drops of Chamomile.

Feet:

FOOT ACHES
General aches or inflammation of the foot
Essential oils: Juniperberry 1 drop; Lavender 3 drops; Peppermint 1 drop
Carrier: GRAPESEED & WHEATGERM BLEND 10 ml
Treatment: A deep, penetrating massage of the feet using the above oils will be very beneficial. Use all the strokes detailed in Chapter 9 for the feet. Treat as necessary.

There are many other conditions that will respond well to massage, particularly if you incorporate essential oils into the treatment. You will usually find that massage is often useful for physical conditions, although many psychological or emotional disturbances can be alleviated by holistic massage. Skin conditions are, generally, less successfully treated with direct massage on the affected areas, but will benefit from a general massage. You can also use a carrier oil with added essential oils gently applied to the affected areas and surroundings.

Using the treatments index detailed on the previous pages you should be able to find a treatment to suit your condition even though it is not listed here.

Further reading

Arnould-Taylor, W. E. *The Principles & Practice of Physical Therapy* (Stanley Thornes Ltd)

Chambers, Philip & Burke, Lisa *The Very Essence: A Guide to Aromatherapy* (Likisma Presentations)

Davis, Patricia *Aromatherapy: an A-Z* (C. W. Daniel Co Ltd)

Gray, Henry *Gray's Anatomy* (Magpie Books Ltd)

Maxwell-Hudson, Clare and others *The Book of Massage* (Ebury Press) *Aromatherapy Massage Book* (Dorling Kindersley)

Mitchell, Stewart *Massage, A Practical Introduction* (Element)

Ryman, Daniele *Aromatherapy* (Piatkus)

Sellar, Wanda *The Directory of Essential Oils* (C. W. Daniel Co Ltd)

Wildwood, Christine *Holistic Aromatherapy* (Thorsons)

Worwood, Valerie Ann *The Fragrant Pharmacy* (Bantam Books)

Useful addresses

ITEC (International Therapy Examination Council)
James House, Oakelbrook Mill, Newent, Glos GL18 1HD

IPTI (Independent Professional Therapists International)
97 London Road, Retford, Notts DN22 7EB

City & Guilds of London Institute
76 Portland Place, London W1N 4AA

The Northern Institute
100 Waterloo Road, Blackpool Lancs FY4 1AW

The Shiatsu Society
19 Langside Park, Kilbarchan Renfrewshire PA10 2EP

International Institute of Reflexology
PO Box 34, Harlow, Essex

Contact your local college for details of courses in Massage or Aromatherapy.